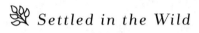 *Settled in the Wild*

ALSO BY Susan Hand Shetterly

Settled in the Wild

Notes from
the Edge of Town

Susan Hand Shetterly

ALGONQUIN BOOKS OF CHAPEL HILL 2010

Published by
ALGONQUIN BOOKS OF CHAPEL HILL
Post Office Box 2225
Chapel Hill, North Carolina 27515-2225

a division of
WORKMAN PUBLISHING
225 Varick Street
New York, New York 10014

Library of Congress Cataloging-in-Publication Data
Shetterly, Susan Hand, [date]
   Settled in the wild : notes from the edge of town /
   Susan Hand Shetterly. — 1st ed.
        p. cm.
   ISBN 978-1-56512-618-3
   1. Natural history — Maine — Anecdotes.   2. Wildlife
   watching — Maine — Anecdotes.   I. Title.
   QH105.M2S54 2010
   508.741 — dc22   2009030802

10 9 8 7 6 5 4 3 2 1
First Edition

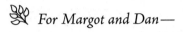 *For Margot and Dan—*

in admiration

What must a man do to be at home in the world?
There must be times when he is here
as though absent, gone beyond words into the woven
    shadows
of the grass and the flighty darknesses
of leaves shaking in the wind ...

                    from "The Silence" by Wendell Berry

❧ Contents

❀ Acknowledgments

I must first thank my gifted, beloved children, Aran Shetterly and Caitlin Shetterly, who allowed me to write about them, supported my work on this book, and who are excellent readers and editors. Without them, I would have few stories to tell.

A profound thanks to Andra Miller, my perceptive, generous, patient editor, and to my agent, David McCormick, who believed in this book and in me.

To my talented readers who have persevered through versions of this manuscript: Cynthia Thayer, Ken Mason, Pam Chodosh, Maggie Hand Miller, Rebecca McCall, Monica Wood, Terry Tempest Williams, and Robert and Rita Kimber. I give you my love and thanks.

To Osmond Bonsey, Mike Benjamin, Sandy Bolster,

Brad Allen, Bruce Connery, and Cherie Mason for sharing their knowledge and ideas.

To Mark McCullough, premier biologist, who gave his time and expertise to answer my questions. I cannot thank him enough.

To Paula and Norman Mrozicki, Margret Baldwin, Susan and Hugh Curran, Dhyana Bisberg, David Page, Mary and John and Mary Furth, Nancy Hathaway, and Nancy and Andy Kandutsch for their work to preserve and steward our precious lands on the Morgan Bay watershed, and for their nurturing friendships.

To Susan and Charles Guilford, Mary and Steve Hildebrand, Sue Straubing, Ruth and Jim Yerkes, and Mariah Hughs and Nick Sichterman, for their love of place. To Ray McDonald for allowing me to write about him. To Wilbur Saunders for his careful edit, and to Anne and David McGraw for their decision to save Jed Island from development. To the staff and the board of Blue Hill Heritage Trust, especially to Jim Dow and Pam Johnson, who taught me how to think about land and how to work to save it. Their intelligence and hard work have given me inspiration and an education.

Acknowledgments

To those teachers who live on in memory: Marion Stocking, Naomi Church, Jack Dudley, Chandler Richmond, Laredo Carter, and Philip Booth.

To the memory of my mother, Dorothy, my father, Trav, my mother-in-law, Birdie, and my father-in-law, Pop. They are the scaffolding of my life. Whatever I have become, I have built from their support.

And lastly, to the gift of wildness in the lands where I have made my home—in Prospect Harbor and in Surry—and to the many lives they shelter. I owe them just about everything.

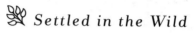 *Settled in the Wild*

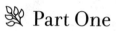 Part One

April Nights

🌿 I leave a window open on April nights and put my pillow close to that cold slice of air because I want to hear spring come back to this small clearing. Sometimes it snows and I hear that soft muffled falling, or it sleets and I hear instead the sharp tick of ice against the glass. But mostly the sounds are new.

One night a flock of Canada geese flew north under the half-moon. I woke to their bugling from the south and listened as the birds crossed over the roof, close enough to catch the sound of their wings like a bow drawn back and forth across the bass strings of a cello.

Maybe ten geese. Maybe fifteen. An uneasy silence followed as if the thrust of their heraldic flight had upset the air behind them, as if they had broken through the glaze of winter above my house and trailed spring's upheaval and promise.

After midnight, a porcupine climbed into the weeping willow by the frog pond and started to snip off the young branches, tender and crisp with new leaves and swelling buds. I heard one branch, then another, slip through the branches below them and land on the ground with an almost inaudible sigh. Lying under a pile of quilts, I counted the falling branches. When I got to five, I forced myself up in the dark, turned on the kitchen light, and stepped outside. The light sparkled on the frosted grass beneath the tree. I was barefoot, wearing an old T-shirt. Another branch dropped as I walked in the dark to the driveway, picked up a handful of stones, and pitched them in the direction of the tree. They bounced off the trunk, splashing into the frog pond through paper-thin ice.

In the moonlight I could see the dark blob of porcupine against the sky. It was pressing itself against the trunk, about twenty-five feet up, like a big irregular fruit stuck in the branches. I tossed a few more stones.

"That's for eating my tree!" I said.

Back in bed, as clearly as if the porcupine were answering the force of my assault, I heard another branch drop.

An hour or so later, a loon flew over. It filled the night with one long cry. What the voice said was that the ice is starting to melt off the nearby lakes, almost enough to give loons the open water they need. What the voice said was that it could hardly wait.

Just before dawn, a raccoon, perhaps the first to rise from its restless winter sleep, began to sort through the shed. I must have left the door ajar. I listened as it tossed aside what was probably a wine bottle out of the recycling bin. Then the empty plastic compost bucket rolled across the shed floor. Then something heavy dropped. I wasn't sure. Maybe one of my son's old winter boots that I wear around the yard, now that he's grown up and gone.

Everything in that cold predawn was exquisitely quiet except for this one raccoon, the only soul in the universe making noise.

Going Back to the Land

The idea that we were going back to the land made me laugh. It was the word *back*. With our son, who was less than a year old, my husband and I moved into an unfinished cabin on a sixty-acre woodlot in downeast Maine with no electricity, no plumbing, no phone. It was June 1971.

We had both grown up in suburbs. This was all new. And I laughed with relief when we survived the first year.

I am old enough now to sympathize with my parents-in-law when they arrived for a visit in the fall of that year, just on the lip of serious snow. We were filled with all we had half-learned in our hardworking brand-new lives and we couldn't wait to share it. They entered our little cabin in the evening, an interior illuminated by lamps that held their kerosene brightness close and threw shadows across the room. My mother-in-law slipped off her mink coat and draped it over a chair.

When we sat down to a dinner of mashed rutabaga and soy burgers, brown rice and parsnips, my father-in-law, who had brought his own bottle of gin and was refilling his glass as if it contained oxygen and he had been blasted against his will to the moon, looked up at me through a startled haze as I set a warm loaf of whole wheat bread on the table. "Everything's beige," he growled.

Before I could begin to explain why I thought beige was good for him, a skunk, living beneath the floorboards of the kitchen, released an explosion of spray, and the mink coat got a dose of its old life back.

As a young child, I thought that the stories I loved were a birthright of sorts. I thought they were about what my life would be. My entitlement. *Little House on the Prairie. Charlotte's Web, Huckleberry Finn, The Last of the Mohicans.* Then, on television, Hopalong Cassidy, and then the movie *Shane.* So, where was the prairie? The farm? The river? The deep woods and high outcrops? The men who rode in from behind the dark mountain to make things make sense? They did not make sense. I lived in an apartment on Bleecker Street in New York City with my mother and father and sister and a series of turtle pets brought home in little cardboard boxes every year from the Barnum and Bailey circus. My mother took me to church and to the zoo. My father took me, for company, to the White Horse Tavern.

This was not my narrative of choice. Clearly, I had been adopted by misfits. But when my father's fortunes rose, he bought us a house in Westport, Connecticut, with five acres of fields and woods, and I felt I was going home: my first time going back to the land I had never come from. I was eight years old.

I recall the polite men who came to carry our furniture down the carpeted stairs of the apartment building and out to a van, and how my father invited friends—the woman, a buyer for Lord and Taylor, and her husband, a city lawyer—to accompany us as we drove in our new car out to our new eighteenth-century country home. I was excited to the point of breathlessness. My most recent turtle was well into its decline, floating listlessly in a bowl of cloudy water on the floor of the back seat.

Sporting a derby set rakishly on his head, my father drank from a silver flask and sang his favorite songs.

K-K-K-Katy, beautiful Katy,
You're the only, only g-g-g-girl that I adore,
When the m-m-m-moon shines over the c-c-c-cowshed,
I'll be waiting at the k-k-k-kitchen door.

My younger sister and I yelled out the words. We threw back our heads, laughing.

My mother sat quiet and pale. Her husband had no idea how to drive a car. He was going to kill us.

When we arrived, my father aimed the car alongside a stone wall that bordered the big lawn in front of our new house. The car jerked and stalled. My sister lost her balance, jamming her foot into the turtle bowl. The coup de grâce.

Everyone but me leapt out. I heard doors thrown open, windows raised, footsteps rattling up and down the stairs of the big old colonial. From the back seat, I heard my mother's happy voice exclaiming.

I picked up the bowl, walked into the field beyond the house, and took my time scraping out a burial hole with my fingers. Setting the dead turtle into the rich-smelling dirt, I gave it a prayer and covered it up.

This was not the worst way to enter the life I had longed for: hidden in the tall plants, digging at the dirt, releasing a small animal who probably would have, had it lived, recognized this smell and these plants as the primary stuff of its true narrative.

My husband and I moved into the cabin, turned over dirt, hoed it up, and planted a garden. We celebrated our son's first birthday. The three of us slept on a mattress on the floor. We built screens, stuck them into the window frames, and left the old rummage-sale windows open at night. I had never heard a whippoorwill, but here it woke us as it sang from its chosen rock by the front door. We crept to a window and held our son up to see the bird crouched against the round gray granite. The blast of its chanting enveloped us, and we listened for the little click between the chants as if it were clearing its throat.

Our child, framed in the moonlight, was fully attentive. He would grow up with the woods, the subsistence gardens, the working harbor and its fishermen, the harsh winters and the brilliant and brief summers. He would be from somewhere.

As a child I had not been taught the things that would connect me to the land. My parents could not teach what they did not know and what did not interest them at that point in their busy lives.

But there is something to be said for the benign neglect in which I was raised in Connecticut: it gave me freedom. No one seemed to be worried about my getting hurt or lost or kidnapped. I just wandered away and wandered back again. The land around the house offered the space and the privacy to act out the stories I loved. Even when my best friend, Susie Campbell, and I made ourselves bows and arrows and built an Indian camp and thatched it with the leaves of a poison sumac bush and were sick for a week with rashes on the insides of our eyelids and undersides of our tongues—our faces so horribly swollen, we hardly recognized each other— my parents never restricted me. Not even when I discovered a thick gray snake coiled on a rock on the dry bed of Farm Brook, nudged it with a stick, and reported to them that it had raised its head and hissed, did they seem unduly upset. The world about the house was open to me and I was making it mine as best I could.

I imagine my mother watching from the kitchen window as I headed off into the woods once more, a sturdy, slight kid, dressed in old clothes and rubber boots, striding all by herself into the trees. There was a time, I knew, when my mother had been an adventurer. She had hiked all alone on Cape Cod, following Thoreau's maps.

What she wanted for me I do not know, but I imagine she did not want surprises. Where was this girl going? My mother was beginning to see her first child as a person entire, someone who had the capacity to sabotage her hopes for a respectable, maybe even charming, daughter.

I was gone, and she did not see me drawing away the

previous fall's clotted leaves from the thread of water that ran through the springtime oaks and hickories. It was a self-appointed task I took seriously, digging my numbed fingers into wads of leaves, watching the water rise and pearl and run. Once I found a red salamander, so cold it was hardly able to move, and I held the bright stunned animal for a time in my hand.

A number of years later, when I no longer went into the woods to clean out the leaves from running water, I read Robert Frost's poem "The Pasture," which begins:

> I'm going out to clean the pasture spring;
> I'll only stop to rake the leaves away

I thought he had been watching me doing what I needed to do then and that perhaps I had not been entirely alone. Or, I thought, perhaps helping water run free is something many people long to make happen. I discovered, reading the poem, that I had been right all along: stories are about us.

In our cabin two miles from a working harbor, my son learned as we learned, and for us everything was new.

What will happen to us when our children have no connection with what is wild in the land, its depth, danger, generosity? What will life be like for children who do not grow up paying close attention to it and testing themselves against it? And what will happen to those children who ache for it, as I did, but cannot find it anywhere?

We humans evolved along with other species. We became who we are by figuring out who they were: prey, predator, and the thousands of other important things in between. We weren't just looking at something, we were participating in community. We were the soft clay. The wild world was the potter's wheel and the potter's hand.

Who will we become, when only witchgrass, gray squirrels, herring gulls, Norway rats, and others like them conduct their astonishingly adaptable lives outside our houses? Will we live as hostages to what we have made, stunned by loneliness and homesick for what we can no longer even imagine?

⌄

In those early years in Maine, various people who wanted to try an alternative lifestyle wandered into our lives. Those of us who were settling in sometimes found a stranger or two knocking at the door for a meal or a place to sleep. I remember one thin boy who had just graduated from Harvard turning down our invitation to dinner because, he said, although he drank water, he believed that the need for food had not been conclusively established, and he wanted to test the truth of it. He slept in his car in the driveway and left before dawn. We never saw him again.

For a few summers, a rather charming, dissolute man from New York City sold the clams he dug from the bays around the harbor up on Route 1. He parked on the side of the highway, threw open the trunk of his car where he kept his wooden hods chock-full of clams, and sat in the driver's seat, smoking pot, waiting for tourists. The clams died in the heat, an oozing, stinking mess. When we warned him that if someone were stupid enough to buy them, they would get sick, he insisted that the clams were just resting.

Our back-to-the-land lives started out rarified, idealistic, dangerously unprepared, and, frankly, arrogant. We may have brought with us inner resources for a certain amount of isolation and for living poor, but our fortunes turned on how we adjusted to our new community. We removed ourselves from a culture we knew and set ourselves down into something that required hard physical work, patience, and the ability to pay close attention. Those of us who thrived here learned from the land and from our neighbors. And, over time, we were changed.

I sometimes bundled up my son in late summer, and we went out in the cold early morning to the mudflats where my husband dug clams. He sold them to a family in town who shucked them, packed them in ice, and drove them down the coast to sell to restaurants for chowders and fried clam plates. At low tide, the big rocks stood high on the cobbled shore. As my husband dug, my son and I explored under the wet, gelatinous fronds of rockweed, finding whelk eggs, northern periwinkles, green crabs, and brittle and northern stars.

One morning, driving on a dirt road toward one of the flats, we were startled by a woman who darted in front of us waving her arms. We stopped and got out of the truck to see what the problem was.

"You can't come in here!" she announced.

"Why not?" my husband asked.

"It's private property," she said. Behind her stood a lovely summerhouse with a front porch that looked out to Gouldsboro Bay.

"We're just driving to the beach," my husband told her. "I dig clams and the low-tide beach isn't private land."

"But not through here you don't," she said, slamming her fists into her hips. "Not down this road you don't. We've got grandchildren who play on the road."

I shifted the weight of my son from one arm to the other.

"Excuse me," I said. "We've got a child, too."

She stared at me for a moment, then said, "Well, just this once."

The years passed, and we grew into our home place. In the summers my mother came to visit, and in anticipation, my son gathered his favorite books and put them in a pile next to the bed in the loft where she slept. When the first light of morning filled the windows, he would tiptoe out of bed, climb up, and snuggle in with her. Sometimes, when I brought her coffee, I'd find them asleep together, their heads leaning against one another. They took long, leisurely times in the loft. Working downstairs, I would hear the drift of my mother's voice reading the words in the books my son knew by heart.

My mother had cancer. My father was spending his time in psychiatric hospitals. These were people who had shone like bright stars for years for many, including their two daughters. But my mother was slipping away, all of that particular and dramatic brightness gone. Instead, she was soft and loving to this child who loved her back fiercely. She was the same to my daughter, who was born when she was even sicker, and on whom she doted, as if this girl would carry into the future something of the person she had been and the person she had wanted to become.

Once, when she was visiting and much weaker than before, I came back from weeding the garden and found her emerging with some difficulty from the outhouse, which stood in a patch of goldenrod at the edge of the woods.

"Hi," she said, giving me her big smile. I stared at her.

"Mom," I said, "do you have goldenrod flowers in your nose?"

"Oh," she said, "perhaps I do."

She pulled out the tiny yellow flowers she had stuffed in her nose to protect her from the smell of the outhouse. She smiled at me again and continued up to the house.

That was the first time I cried for us.

Walking at Dusk

Ida Hinkley lived in an old cape about a half a mile from our land, the only other house along the road for a few miles in each direction. She was in her eighties and not at all interested in us as neighbors.

I used to watch her when I worked cutting herring in the canning factory at the harbor. Below her cotton print dress her calves were as muscled as a runner's, and on her head she wore a red wig.

In the spring of our second year, I picked up a jelly clump of wood frog eggs from one of the soaks around the cabin, and we raised them in a two-gallon glass jar.

When they sprouted legs, I released them back to the pools. My two-year-old son and I were fond of those eggs, fascinated by their transformation into polliwogs. In the town library I read about how the undersides of the eggs are white at first, and how that whiteness is the yolk from which the embryos feed. The dark tops of the eggs absorb heat, which encourages the cells to divide. Polliwogs have a breathing pore on their left side, and, at one point of the metamorphosis, they have both lungs and gills.

The best algae for them to eat grew in a ditch by the road in front of Ida's house. Despite the puzzle as to why algae by her house grew in such luxury, I used to walk over with a bucket and collect a bit of it to feed to the polliwogs in the jar and to those in the surrounding pools as well.

One day Ida came home as I was gathering. She stopped her car beside me and rolled down the window.

"Hi, Ida," I said, turning around. "Is it okay if I take some of this to feed to polliwogs?" I held up a strand of green algae for her to admire. She rolled her window shut and glowered at me through the glass.

I leaned over, scooping another handful of the bright green scum, listening as the window unrolled behind me.

"Ida," I said, standing and turning to face her. But she rolled her window up again. She frowned through the glass. Her mouth puckered as if she were sucking a sour ball.

"I'm assuming," I said, leaning toward her, raising my voice through the wall of glass, "that's a 'No'?"

I picked up the bucket and started for home. She drove beside me at about four miles an hour as I walked, escorting me to the edge of her property. Then she turned the car around and parked in front of her old outhouse in her yard. I watched her get out of the car. The outhouse, I thought suddenly. That was the secret of her prizewinning algae.

The winter after my daughter was born, I would set her in her carrier, put it on my back, and take her in the afternoons, before dusk, into the woods. I believed that even if she fell asleep, which she always did, the trees, the tracks of wild animals in the snow, the dead leaves rattling on the branches, the hoot of an owl, a grouse feeding on birch catkins—everything—would pass into her life and make it good. I felt her hot breath at my ear at first, as she babbled and bounced and my boots broke the snow crust in a steady, brittle rhythm. But gradually her breathing became regular and deep and she fell asleep, and I tramped out of the woods and along the back of Ida's field, beyond the view of the house.

That big field was an old pasture, silent in the early evening snow. Apple trees as sturdy and gnarled as Ida herself stuck up into the sky where a ridge dropped to meet them. One of the best things I could think to give my child was this: the woods first, then to emerge from their whisper and shadow onto the smooth clean sweep of Ida's field in winter just before dark.

These are gifts that last. Small, as easy as breathing in and out, as plain as bread, they sink beneath what we think we remember, what we think we know, but they remain.

Sonny's Song

🌿 One September afternoon when my son was five years old, he walked down the driveway to the small sandpit we owned and then walked back to find me in the chicken shed I had turned into a study. He came in cradling his right hand in his left. I took it into mine and saw that the tip of his index finger was smeared with blood.

"A cricket bit me," he said.

"I don't think crickets bite," I reassured him. He glanced at his finger. How could this reassure him? He had a bloody finger. He had a mother who dispensed facts about the known world. Although he was starting to find his way on his own, it was an errant path, and he needed help knowing what was true and what was not.

I washed his hand, taped his finger with a Band-Aid, and we headed to the sandpit together. The shallow quarter-acre scoop was an old moraine. On one side grew a fringe of young maples and beech trees. In the summer, their leaves threw moving shadows across the sand. The pit had not been commercially dug for years, and raspberry brambles and grasses and other pioneer vegetation had filled in at the edges, but there was plenty of open sand left in the middle. Dark algae ringed a scrape that held a couple of inches of water for a day or so after a hard rain, when songbirds came to drink and to bathe in it. Wolf spiders and jumping spiders lived on the sand, and so did turquoise tiger beetles. Antlion larvae buried themselves, digging tunnels to the surface and waiting at the bottom of them with the tips of their long pincers exposed. My son and I had seen all this, and we had also witnessed ferocious wars when the red-and-black ants that lived on the side of the pit swept down in Biblical armies to overwhelm the black ants of the plain.

That particular September, when the maple leaves turned red, drifting down a few at a time, and the wind rattled the beech leaves tight to their branches, we dug two holes in the sand with a trowel and laid old boards across them. We wanted to catch a cricket. We had read they make good pets.

He pointed to the hole. We knelt down and looked in. Pieces of cricket legs, a half-eaten grasshopper, and a ground beetle's head and wings lay strewn over the bottom. On top of them stood a shiny black male field cricket. I assumed that my son had nicked his finger on one of the boards. I had not heard of crickets biting. But my confidence wavered. How, I wondered, did all those body parts get in there?

"I'll catch him," I said. "And then you can hold him. You'll see he doesn't bite."

"Okay," he answered, but it was clear this was not his idea of a good plan. I reached in. The cricket took a quick jump back. When it latched on to my finger, I whipped my hand out of the hole and screamed, and my son fell backward onto the sand.

"They do bite!" he shouted, righting himself.

We stared at the blood running down my finger.

"Wow!" he said. And, very gently, he smiled.

In a cracked aquarium we made a sand and pebble home for the cricket. My son scooped him up with a measuring cup and shook him into it, then I carried the whole thing to the house and set it in my son's room on a table by the bed.

Two weeks before, he had started kindergarten. He decided to name the cricket "Sonny" after the bus driver.

"Why Sonny?" I asked.

He said, "Because Sonny's big."

"Right," I said.

He dropped a jar lid into the aquarium for Sonny to hide under during the day, and fed him flakes of oatmeal and bits of lettuce. At night he fell asleep to loud chirps.

All winter and into the spring Sonny stepped from beneath that lid in the dark to scrape his wings together.

I don't know what this winter singing meant to him. He lived long after his fellow crickets dropped in the killing frosts, and he never drew a rival or a mate.

For me, Sonny's song was a reminder that the bigger world is where our children are always headed. A sand-pit is just a place to start from.

All this happened a long time ago, but I remember standing at the doorway of my son's bedroom at night, drawn by the bright, harsh singing. The snow piled up outside. Sometimes the moon shone in through the windows with a fierce light. It illuminated Sonny, casting his sharp silhouette onto his patch of sand.

A cricket taught my son that mothers don't know everything, even when they say they do. My boy's waking hours were dense with the yellow school bus, the big driver, the schoolhouse, its play yard, other children, their parents, and the teachers who guided him into new discoveries. At night he fell asleep to Sonny's song. It was a musical footbridge of sorts that strung itself between innocence and experience, a tenacious little bridge that was taking him across.

Dangers

✻ Elaine Lowell looked through the north-facing window of her house, down the hill, past the cannery parking lot, to the little sand cove at the harbor. It was a day when sea fog was rising off the water because the water, which was cold enough to kill a person, was warmer than the air. The sea fog moved this way and that, parting like a gauzy curtain, and there on the sand lay something dark. A seal, maybe. But not a harbor seal. They swim south in the winter. Perhaps it was one of those big northern seals, the ones they call horseheads. The tide was coming in, and that big seal was inching ever so slowly just ahead of the rising water. Then she saw her husband's dory poking its bow into the sand behind the animal, its stern drifting sideways, and she knew she wasn't watching a seal at all.

"If you hadn't caught sight of me, the tide would have swallowed me up. No doubt about it," George told her. "No doubt about it, I would have drowned," he said. An ambulance rushed him to the hospital, where doctors discovered that the vertebrae in his lower back had compressed and cracked, and they informed him his seaworthy days were gone.

The fishermen who moored their boats in the inner harbor of our town were like acrobats who worked without safety nets. What kept them alive was their expertise and their sense of community from boat to boat. What endangered them was a slight mishap, a chance mistake, an error of judgment. They did not believe in learning how to swim. They had no use for it. Where would swimming get them? They were loaded down with rubber boots and clothing that would sink them before the cold water made it too hard to move. Swimming just postponed things. Swimming was a summer diversion, something done from shore, something for those who had free time. The fishermen of this harbor knew the water. They rode its back as if they were setting one foot ahead of the other on a taut wire, as if they were launching themselves daily into a double somersault and reaching out to catch a trapeze. No safety net.

The reality of death made them ironic; their sense of life made them tough, cocky, independent, and, sometimes, contemptuous.

$$\curlyvee$$

"You don't want to see a man after he's been in the water a while," the marine warden told me. "You don't want to know what the crabs and the whelks do to a dead man."

The crabs and the whelks? The same Jonah crabs the fisherman took as bycatch in their lobster traps and gave us for free when we hurried down to the docks with our buckets? The same crabs we carried home in those buckets and boiled and picked the sweet meat out of and mixed with mayonnaise and ate on Triscuits? The same whelks Elaine and Susan and the other women at the harbor pickled in vinegar and stored in jars on their shelves, the same whelks they popped in their mouths every now and then, or chopped up and added to pasta sauce?

Yes. The answer—in both cases—was yes.

My husband and I did not make our living on the water. He dug clams. We gathered windrows of seaweed for our garden. Our son fished for mackerel down at the cannery, standing on the riprap on shore, and our daughter liked to wander the beaches collecting the bleached, calcareous tests of sea urchins and the red and green and yellow rubber bands that washed up from the boats of lobstermen who used them to clamp the claws of lobsters. We were littoral people, waders, summertime swimmers who spent hours beside the water and short spurts in it, and breathed in its smell that blew into our woodlot, that bitter, life-giving astringency. Because I was not a fisherman or the wife of a fisherman, the water did not scare me.

⌄

Danny Mitchell owned a garbage business in town. He hired a man by the name of Clarence for our run: the harbor and Pond Road, Tuesdays. One day I walked down our long driveway to retrieve the empty can and found, resting its blade against the back of our mailbox post and its handle in the grass, a mended sickle. We had tossed a broken one into the garbage can. I saw Clarence the next day and asked him about it.

"Oh," he said. "Danny fixed it. He doesn't believe much in throwing things away."

We lived in a town where the garbageman didn't think much of throwing things away. He retrieved our sickle, soldered it, returned it, and we used it for years. I still have it.

Clarence was young, thin, wiry, and dark-haired. He held two jobs. He worked for Danny and he worked on a boat as a stern man, baiting lobster traps, then tossing them over. He died a month after he set that sickle in the grass.

A trap has a chunk of cement in it to weight it. Out on the boat Clarence threw a trap overboard and its rope slithered and kinked and snatched his ankle. It whipped him over the side and yanked him underwater. He died upside down.

You would not have wanted to see him when they found him. You remembered him the way he was on shore: dark-haired, hardworking, quick.

Edith, a woman of excellent reputation, was in charge of the school lunch program. She was small, a little bit bent over, and wore her white hair short and curled. I met her when I taught at the local elementary school and noticed right away her kindness for every child.

One afternoon in spring, I stayed late to work on papers. I had spread them across a table in the cafeteria, and Edith came out of the kitchen, wiping her hands on her apron, and sat down to chat with a classroom aid who was her neighbor. Her husband arrived to drive her home. He was a handsome man. He stood behind her, one hand on the back of her chair, talking to the janitor.

I raised my eyes from my work to look at him and saw his head bathed in window light. He looked like a beautiful photograph of himself.

After a while, he drove Edith home. The afternoon wore on. I finished my work and left the school.

Sometime later that spring his boat went missing. For two days every boat in the harbor fleet was out searching. The town held its breath. I held the picture of his head bathed in light.

Edith came to work. She put on her hairnet and apron, organized the kitchen, and fed the children their lunches. When I asked her why she was doing all this, she said, "If I stayed home, I'd worry too much."

His boat had drifted into an island cove. He was found by his friends lying on his back, one leather glove on, one off. He had suffered a heart attack.

"I am thankful," said Edith quietly, "he did not die in the water."

$$\curlyvee$$

To the north of town lay a broad marsh where salt hay had been cut in the nineteenth century. An old sod dike, worn by time and storms, ran along the outer edge in front of the tidal water. It was a big place, a few miles long and a mile or so across, full of grasses and channels, rimmed by woodland. I visited often, standing at the border in the woods, with my binoculars trained on the marsh, looking for birds.

One January, when it had turned to ice, I walked it. The wind shot it down like handfuls of thrown tacks and the top layers of salty ice shattered under my pack boots, but the lower, thicker levels held, and I walked to the old dike and back. The only thing I found was a dead minnow, its silver body as hard as a skipping stone, its eyes like tiny blue marbles. It bumped along the ice, pushed by the wind.

Then, the next year, one afternoon before hard frost, I decided to hike across the marsh. I stepped out onto it and a group of blue-winged teal took off, flashing white underwings, flying in a tight band, settling into a far channel. As I walked, I raised sparrows that flew ahead of me and dropped quickly into the grass. They were fast and secretive, like mice. I sat down on the damp ground to watch them. A group of Canada geese stood in the distance like figures in a crèche. My presence had made them freeze. But the distance between us seemed acceptable to them—my sitting down, even more so—and they began to move among each other after a while, a small band of migrating birds. Around me the hidden sparrows called back and forth. When I stood up again, the geese took off with a lot of running and honking, their feet stomping across the grass and splashing through the salt pools, their long necks outstretched.

The marsh channels wound from the streams in the woods to the bay. Most had narrow bottlenecks I could jump across, but some had gone back to the shape they were before the dike prevented the transformative action of storms and spring tides, which left them wide and quite deep, and especially soft with mud. That day the tide was dead low, and the channels held only a slurry of water.

It wasn't that I hadn't heard stories about bloodworm diggers caught with their gear in marsh channels when a tide rushed in and the water overwhelmed them. But the stories seemed apocryphal. Where did tides like that build so quickly? And why didn't the men drop their gear and scramble out of the mud and up the bank? It didn't make sense.

When I came to a channel that was too wide to jump, I decided to step into it and slog across. The sides gleamed with finely granulated mud, and in the center lay an innocent catchment of mud-colored water. On the far side, the slant up was gradual and the bank above it dense with Spartina grasses. I walked in, taking giant steps in my high rubber boots. The mud sucked at the boots. I continued down. Another step and I could not budge either foot. Maybe this is how it started for the bloodworm diggers, I thought, rather casually. I leaned forward and pulled hard to release myself. I could not move.

Nowhere—not on these marshes or in the coves or out along the mudflats—is it a good idea to trivialize the power of the water. But I didn't know this quite yet. I stood sinking and stuck, aware all at once how alone I was.

What a stupid way to die, I said to myself, and yanked again. The more I yanked, the deeper I went. I thought of my children, my husband. What would they say to this? I missed them achingly.

In a rage, I tossed the binoculars up into the grass, tore my feet out of the boots, and began to crawl. Mud took my elbows, shoulders, knees, neck, my chin. I was swimming in it, trying not to thrash, and managed to grab a handful of grass and then another. I started to pull myself out with a nasty puckering sound as my legs came free. I climbed up the bank and turned to see, down in the middle of the channel, the cuff of one boot in the silty water. Wild with relief, I grabbed the binoculars and walked in my socks to the trees.

As I circled the edge of marsh and the trees, I sang, and what came out first was "Red River Valley" and then "Rock of Ages," and then I sang them all over again at the top of my lungs. It was my own voice I needed to hear. In ruined socks, I strode the long curve of the marsh edge to the car. Birds took off around me. I didn't care.

Plastered in mud, bone-cold, unrecognizable to anyone but myself, I loved my life.

The Inward Eye

It is a rainy morning, the first week of May, good weather to plant nasturtiums. I sit on the porch steps with rubber boots on, a baseball cap, and a slicker, holding the packages of seeds I bought at the feed store in town yesterday. The rain is steady and cold, the light is steel gray, and the yard is patchy and wet. But the pictures on the packages vibrate with color. Nothing looks as good as these nasturtium flowers right now: deep red, eye-jolting orange, electric yellow.

Absentmindedly, I begin to recite William Wordsworth's "I Wandered Lonely as a Cloud" to myself.

I have known the poem by heart ever since my father taught it to me when I was a child:

> For oft, when on my couch I lie
> In vacant or in pensive mood,
> They flash upon the inward eye
> Which is the bliss of solitude;
> And then my heart with pleasure fills,
> And dances with the daffodils.

Wordsworth's inner eye saw daffodils. I say the poem and see hummingbirds. The nasturtiums are for them, and planting the flowers is my gesture of faith that they will come back to my yard once more. As I rip open the packages and push the seeds into the dirt, I know that these tiny bright-colored nectar-drinking birds, each of whom weighs only a few grams—about the weight of four or five of these seeds—have already whirred in erratic flocks across five hundred miles of open water, running the Gulf of Mexico in a twenty-six-hour heat.

Hummers do exactly what physiologists once insisted they could not do. A bird that weighs so little, they argued, cannot go from the Yucatán to the mouth of the Big Muddy without a refueling stop. Such a dot of a bird cannot carry the extra fat it needs to get across all that water. Halfway, the birds should self-destruct, should burn up and fall like a cloud of cinders. But now we know that they can carry the fat they need, and they do. Instead of burning up, they land in the antebellum gardens of the South, pooped, drooped, and alive. And another spring has begun.

The ruby-throat is the only species of hummingbird that always turns east, that always comes north. One thousand miles to Surry, Maine. They will be here as the nasturtiums put out their first brave leaves.

Hummers are built for heat and the sweet profusion of flowers. Their fall migrations draw them down into Mexico and Central America, but it astonishes me that a bird this small flies so far north. Home for some of them is right here in this clearing, a precise measure on their internal compasses, and every spring they want it back.

I have read that rubys survive cool Maine nights by falling into torpor, a short hibernation that lowers their body temperatures and slows their metabolisms. Rousing at daylight takes time and the warmth of the sun.

A reptilian adaptation, torpor prevents the birds from starving to death in the dark. The little motors idle. Out cold, and sometimes hanging upside down, they cling with their toes locked to thin branches.

Females brood their newly hatched young in nests smaller than eggcups. I found one once and discovered the two snug nestlings. Featherless, rubbery gray, they looked like ticks after a good feed. No hint of the glittering refulgence to come.

The iridescent reds and greens of the mature bird are tricks played by the feathers, whose structures fracture the sun's rays, causing them to scatter. In shadow, the male hummer's throat is black, but when light is broken against it, the feathers throw back that ruby flash.

A few fossilized bones of hummers have been found in their wintering places. Just a few. Other ancient birds and ferns and shells and insects and flowers and rat-like mammals have pressed their marks into dust and mud in abundance, but the tiny flower pollinators of a million years past have left scant record.

Europeans, who had never seen the birds until they came to the New World, bestowed upon them dazzling names. There is the amethyst-throated sun angel and the glowing puffleg, the black-hooded sunbeam and the blue-throated star frontlet. In France and England, the rich adorned their capes and hats with hundreds of the jewel-like skins. We do not know how many species were lost before we could name them.

In Central America they are called *chupaflores:* flower suckers. A tough-sounding name for a tough and willful bird. A *chupaflor* will challenge hawks and eagles who fly too close to its nest. It scolds snakes and squirrels. A *chupaflor* will try to drive bees and butterflies away from the blossoms it guards. A swaggering, irritable little bird. But it dies in fragile ways. *Chupas* have been swallowed by bullfrogs, gnawed to death by praying mantids, stuck in webs and rolled up by garden spiders, snatched out of the air by dragonflies, gulped down by bass, pronged on thistles.

I lean over, tamping the nasturtium seeds into last year's flowerbed in the rain, and I confess I am worrying. The birds aiming for this wet yard must be over West Virginia by now. Tomorrow they will probably cross those loamy Pennsylvania fields. In a few days, they will have to manage the jagged high-rise landscapes of New York and after that, those of Boston.

They are my daffodils, these birds, and Wordsworth taught us that what dances before the inward eye cannot fail to engage the heart.

Elvers

American eels spawn in the depths of the Sargasso Sea. Then they must die there. No one has seen them spawning or dying. Their decomposing bodies, thousands of them, must tumble in slow motion along the ocean floor, enriching the water beneath the wide mats of floating sargassum.

The translucent eel larvae drift upward and wiggle through the seaweed fronds. That is where biologists find them. They are shaped like tiny beech leaves. They don't look like eels, but rather like minute fishes made out of glass. Drifting and swimming weakly, they move north through the immense, moody Atlantic. Their radish-seed heads store information by which they navigate these huge spaces, and they aim for the place their parents came from. A year or so later, a few of them swim into the salt marsh near my house.

They have changed utterly. From leaf shape, to tiny glass eels, they re-create themselves here as ink-black elvers two or three inches long. I find them burrowing in the grit around rocks. They are the males, most likely. The females head into lakes and ponds to feed and grow for five to ten years or even longer. But the males swim in and out of the surrounding marshes and estuaries and up streams, feeding for a few years until they join schools of other silver-sleek autumn eels traveling into deep salt water, back to the Sargasso Sea to mate and to die.

Many species are born with an immutable attachment to place. Home means everything. To hummingbirds, to eels, to people. I know what it is to lose a home. My mother lost her beautiful old colonial house, which was her safety and her love. I learned from watching her the primal shock. But I also learned from this place in the woods what it is to settle in, to raise children with a sense of where they come from, which helps them define and refine who they are.

When the elvers swim into this neighborhood marsh, I pick one up and it curls through the water in my hands, nudging at the crevasses between my fingers for a way out. I stick my hands into the water again, spread my fingers, and let it go. It swims down and disappears between two pebbles. Gone. Gone home.

Eden

For those of us who ventured into the woods convinced we could re-create Eden in an undamaged place, the years went by and the successes we celebrated were balanced, as they always are, by failures. Couples who thought they held the same values, who thought they loved each other, found that under the pressure of living hard and close and often poor, they did not, and filed for divorce. My husband and I were among them.

But Eden never failed us. We carried within us onto untilled ground the seeds of our own undoing. We also brought our capacity for accomplishment. And we planted them both.

I remember how I loved that first summer. The cabin was an open, simple place, all wood, set in second-growth hardwoods with some large pines and firs that a logger, for some reason, had left. It shared its life with the world outside. It had a red hand pump in the kitchen and an outhouse over in the trees. The land and the cabin—our days pared down to this elemental life and centered in the natural world—gave me myself, as if I had lost a part of who I was somewhere along the way and recognized the familiar rudiments here, in a place I had never been before.

When I look back, what I treasure most are the evenings of deep winter. Dusk spread across the snow as the sun flared and slanted away behind the trees. The dark came after. Around our kitchen table where we set the lanterns, we ate and read and our two children played with crayons and clay as the kettle on the woodstove steamed. We were timeless. Our lives knitted together snugly here, our voices were easy, our sense of being a part of something precious that we had made together, profound.

Treasure

A neighbor called today to tell me that twenty wild turkeys roosted in the spruce by her house last night. It is a tall tree, thickly branched, and each turkey flew up and took its time settling in, finding a particular branch that suited, spacing itself so that it was not overwhelmed by the bulky closeness of another, but not too far from the comforting density of the flock.

She watched this jockeying from her second-story window as the sun slipped behind the rise of land to the west, and saw, in the last reflected light from the sky, the pitch-black forms of the birds deep in the tree, their heads tucked in. She and her husband fell asleep knowing those wild lives slept close by.

The state wildlife department reintroduced turkeys here about twelve years ago. The birds who share this land with us now are not the descendants of the birds that lived here in the 1700s. These came, through a reintroduction program in Vermont, from remnant populations that held on in small pockets in the backwoods of the southern Appalachians. From a two-hundred-year absence, brought on by overhunting and the destruction of the original woodlands, turkeys now thrive in our open woods and cutover land and fields. The winters are milder, the bird feeders, plentiful. These turkeys are doing fine.

One might argue that because they were brought from somewhere else and because they get a boost from our feeders, our birds are an artificial construct, a human indulgence. But watch them for a while. Adaptable, cunning, they are not hothouse birds. They are not tame. They take to this land just as they did before we got here.

In spring, the males perform their dances in our fields

and woods, dragging their wings and fanning their tails, their heads a swollen mottle of powder blue and red. There is nothing quite like the rich mahogany of their iridescent feathers, the drumming staccato as they strop their wings stiffly along the ground, the slow formality of the dance, the sudden aggressive rushes, the infinitely calibrated circling.

Once when I was out walking the Sopkin woods road in high summer, I watched a mother turkey swirl her big wings around her chicks to protect them from my approach, and the gesture, touching and vulnerable, has stayed with me.

So, too, has the image of wet turkeys. I have seen flocks of the drenched birds in cold fall rains crossing my field like grounded pterodactyls.

We give what is wild a chance, and sometimes it comes back, and we are the better for it. Not only you and me, but others. I am thinking of the body of a young hen turkey lying up the hill on the snow on my land. She was killed two nights ago, taken, perhaps, by an owl or a fisher while she was roosting in a spruce by the road. Her head and neck are gone. The yellow corn she ate at my feeder spills from her torn gizzard—gold on the snow. Her breast is flensed and red, and her feathers lie in a dark wreath around her. She is food in the hungriest time of year.

For three years, the state sponsored a hacking program, in which young peregrine falcons were released to the wild from cages built onto the side of Jordan Cliff at Acadia National Park, an hour's drive from here.

Falco peregrinus anatum, a subspecies of peregrine that once nested on our cliffs, is gone from here. We lost it to pesticide poisoning.

Sometimes I see a peregrine charging above the bay below my house in early fall, twisting straight up into the air, sweeping back down across the marsh. It could be a member of the subspecies *tundrius,* which nests far to the north and survived the poisoning. Or it could be one of the descendants of the birds from Jordan Cliff. If so, it is a mix of a number of subspecies. It carries the genes of birds from the high plains of Castile and from the Australian outback. It was bred to fill an empty place.

We live on the coast, a choice that brings with it historical memory. We never saw the virgin trees looming at the edge of the water as the first travelers from across the Atlantic did. Nor did we see flounder and cod so plentiful in the bays that you could scoop them up in a basket, and lobsters as long as a man's forearm prowling the tide pools. We never heard the huge silence under the trees in the filtered light of primeval forest, the sudden explosions of running game. For the people who lived here, this was old land, but for us it was new—it was Eden—the hard, dangerous gift all over again.

Chac

Once upon a time, in the high branches of a spruce, there sat a rough nest with four young ravens in it. Three flourished. One did not. Three grew up and flew, but one did not. The parents fed the bird in the nest now and then, but they spent more time with the healthy birds, and then, one day, they did not return.

The raven in the nest hunkered down. It was alone now, and it mumbled to itself, preened a little bit, and got hungrier. Some nights passed. Some days came and went. One morning the starving bird struggled to the edge of the nest. It launched itself and tumbled to the ground. A hiker found it, carried it out of the woods, and gave it to an old man who had taken good care of wild birds for more than twenty years.

The raven lay in a cardboard box packed with loose straw on the lawn of the old man's place. The man had doctored many birds over the years, but now his vigilance was wearing down. Sometimes birds were brought to him, and he could not make himself do much for them.

"What's wrong with that raven?" I asked.

"I don't know," he said.

"May I take it?"

The old man waved his hand and said, "Go ahead. See what you can do."

In the car, the raven spoke a little—low, sandpapery sounds—which I tried to imitate. It responded, and by the time I pulled into my driveway, we had something of a conversation going. But as I carried the box to the house, the bird fell silent, flattening itself into the reeking straw. I set towels on the kitchen table, took out my emergency kit, and lifted the terrified bird from the box, gently turned it on its back, and laid a washcloth over its face. Its wings, like the ribs of a broken umbrella, flopped open. I felt its breast, the wasted flesh and sharp sternum; felt the wings, the humerus, the radius, and the ulna; manipulated the joints; pressed lightly on the neck and the throat; examined the toes, the food pads; felt the fibula, patella, femur. My finger caught on something on the left femur. The leg was hot and swollen. I shone a flashlight through the feathers and felt again. It was the tip of a strand of monofilament fishing line. Carefully I pulled at it. The raven squawked. I saw that the bird's flesh had grown over the plastic line like a tree's bark that subsumes a twist of barbed wire over the years.

Many species of birds pick up strands of monofilament left by fishermen. They add them to the linings of their nests along with grasses, rootlets, animal hair. As the young move around in a nest, the monofilament can get caught in a wing or on a leg, and it begins to wrap itself and tighten.

I tugged at the plastic line. The raven struggled. I spread my hand over the bird's chest and pulled at the line again. It ripped through the suppurating flesh, unwinding three times before coming free. The leg sprang a leak. Gathering up the bird in one arm, I rushed to the veterinarian who had opened a temporary office down the road. She stanched the bleeding, disinfected the wound, stitched it up with bright green thread, and bandaged it. At home, with the bird on my lap, I dipped my index finger into a glass of water and held it to side of its beak. Drops slid down my finger into its mouth. I fed it a bowl of high-protein mush, a recipe I made for young songbirds, and gave it water again.

This shattered bird weighed almost nothing—a handful of dry sticks. Its poor body was covered in fledgling plumage, as if it could fly above the trees, but it was too frail to move much, too injured to walk. The inside of its mouth still shone with the bright scarlet color of infancy, still gaped for food like a nestling.

I set the bird in a big basket with clean towels, dropped a cotton blanket over the top to keep out drafts, carried the basket to my tiny study, put it on the floor in the corner, and shut the door. The young bird had been through too much to survive, and I was pretty sure it would, mercifully, die during the night.

In the morning, when I opened the study door, I

heard a peculiar sound, that querulous murmur I had tried to imitate the day before. I drew the blanket back and the bird's head popped up, its scarlet maw opened. It shouted for food.

And that's how we began, the raven and I.

It was early summer, and my son was away, working to set up a school for the children of families who would come to rake blueberries on the barrens downeast. My daughter lived at home, consumed by the complexity of being a teenager. In comparison, my life was rather simple. I wrote articles and essays. I took care of a raven and a garden.

The bird and I got to know each other in that small room where it went back to being a nestling. As its strength grew, we talked more. Sometimes I read aloud paragraphs I wasn't quite sure about, and it mumbled along, the cadences of its voice seeming to mimic mine.

I set a green rubber toad in the basket, which it spent a great deal of time pounding with its beak and carrying as it limped and turned and settled back down upon the towels. It liked jabbing at a dog bone, and pulverizing hard-boiled eggs, then delicately nibbling up the stray morsels.

The basket lay in a splay of late morning sun. I left the screened window open so that the sounds of the day swept in. The raven cocked its head to listen. It played with sticks and pebbles—everything I brought was interesting.

"This room stinks!" my daughter informed me. She was right. The raven wafted a dense sour odor. The waxy marrowbones and the sulfurous eggs added their own particular bouquet. I got used to it. I loved the bird's raucous calls that turned our house into sudden bedlam. It sounded to me as if it were screaming "Chac! Chac!" the name of the Mayan rain god who brings life back. I named the bird Chac, our own dark and smelly rain cloud, our bringer of gifts. The bird was a male, but before we even knew that for sure, we called him "he."

One day, after I removed the bandage from his leg, he spotted the green stitching and in a fit of purposeful activity, ripped at it and flung clots of green thread across the room. The blood came spouting down his leg again, and again I rushed him to the vet. This time she used black thread to match his color.

There was something I was avoiding: a question of the raven's right eye. A friend who was an ophthalmologist stopped in to check it. I held Chac on my lap, and my friend peered into the lovely gray-blue left eye, the color of all young ravens' eyes before they mature and turn black. Then he looked at the right one. He stood up, checked his light, and bent down and looked again. He took out a smaller light, and held open the eyelid as Chac struggled.

"Susan," he said. "This guy seems to be missing an eyeball. There's nothing there. It's just lid and socket."

"How did that happen?" I asked.

"I don't know," he said. "I don't know." Then he looked at the blue-gray eye again. "Well," he said, "at least this eye is perfect. He can see just fine with this one."

"What's he going to do with just one eye?"

Ravens are primarily carrion eaters. They scavenge more than they kill. An owl or a hawk or a blue heron or a tern needs two eyes to see depth and to judge distance to catch prey, but maybe a raven could do without that. Maybe a raven could see the world flat and survive.

In the basket in the study, Chac played with a moon snail shell. The game he made for himself was to try to stick his bill in the large aperture. His aim was off by about an inch. But in time his mind began to coordinate with his good eye, making up the difference for his blind side. His aim was adjusting.

I moved Chac into a medium-sized outside cage where he limped across logs and climbed in and out of his basket and spent a lot of time looking at the world through his one eye. Every night, I brought him in.

I had read that the Norse god Odin kept two ravens, one perched on each shoulder. They talked to him. They flew off—these ravens named Memory and Thought—and returned to whisper in his ears all they had learned.

One day I realized I had to make a choice: I could return Chac to the old man, who had big cages for large permanently disabled birds, which I did not, or I could look for some other wild-bird rehabilitator who had good large-bird facilities and liked ravens. But, like Odin, I was held by what Chac had to say. I chose—for both of us—a third option.

I opened the cage. I let Chac walk free.

Letting him go meant that he would never abide a sheltered life. I offered this tamed and crippled wild prince his own ancestral home—bounteous and dangerous.

By the time I opened the door to his cage and he walked out, his aim was perfect. There he stood on the green grass of the yard, a thin, young raven with one eye and a limp. He looked around and mumbled as he always did when something required his special attention. I stood close by.

"Come on, Chac," I said, "let's have a little walk." He mumbled. He headed away from me, straight to the frog pond, and stepped into the shallow water with what seemed astonishment, and stood stock-still. Then his tail began to pump up and down as if he were mating, and his voice got sharper and deeper and much louder, and his head went under and his wings thrashed, and the frog pond exploded in spray. He did this for so long, I was afraid he might keel over and drown, but finally he walked out—soaked through—shook off, and began to preen. Our terrier, Sadie, whom he had watched from the cage, came up and gently sniffed him. He murmured at her and went on preening.

That evening, I lured him into the cage with food and shut the door, then took the food away to prevent raccoons from trying to pry open the door at night and frightening him. I draped a tarp over it and went inside. The cage sat beneath my bedroom window. Before I fell asleep with Sadie beside me, I listened through the regular nighttime sounds for any slight sound from Chac, but he slept peacefully.

The next morning, I went outside and pulled away the tarp. Chac was awake, trying to stuff himself into his water bowl.

Every morning, when I let him out, the first thing he did was bathe. I offered a bowl of food; he ate some and hid the rest for later. I would watch him from the kitchen window as he gathered food into his beak, his throat hanging loose and heavy with it. He would sidle up to a tuft of grass or a tree root or a stone, look furtively around with his good eye, and then gag the entire mess into his hiding place.

Sadie found every one. She was growing fat from his rancid caches.

Sometimes she followed him on his adventures. Watching them—Chac first and Sadie behind him—was a lesson of sorts. Their comfort together moved me. But I didn't know what it was until I read that wolves and ravens practice a rather precise understanding in the far north. They cooperate. The birds are said to alert wolves to the presence of prey, then the wolves allow the ravens to feast on the leftovers of the kill. When both species are sated, they sometimes play. A wolf can and will kill a raven with a lunge and a snap of its jaws, so the play has plenty of peril in it, but it is the ravens who take the chances and set the distances.

What amazed me was that my little terrier was familiar with this. And so was Chac. They were not strangers to each other.

Chac was becoming a part of the everyday shadows

under the trees. He was always busy. I stepped outside and called for him, and he often answered from somewhere in the woods—a sort of hello shout—but he did not stop whatever it was he was doing. With all the exercise he gave himself, he lost his limp.

One windy afternoon when I was working in the garden, Chac screamed. He had stretched out his wings, which he often did, but this time the wind picked him up and he was coasting about a foot above the field. He dropped into the tall wildflowers and seed-head grasses and vanished.

He marched out, but for the next few days kept his wings clamped to his sides.

When he chose his time to fly, he began to teach himself by jumping and giving a flap or two. Jump, flap, flap. Jump, flap, flap.

Each day, he went higher and farther. When he reached tree-branch level, he would head for one of the smaller firs or spruces and crash into it in a tangle. I would run over and retrieve him. Every time he flew he screamed. But the screams were less about fear and more about showing off. He taught himself to turn in tight circles, hover above a chosen rest stop, perch. He flapped just above the trees and circled back. He aimed and landed on branches. In the mornings when I let him out of the cage, he flew screaming with delight.

The inevitable evening came when he would not let me lead him back to the cage. He perched on the wood-shed roof.

"Get down, Chac," I told him.

"Arrahh, Arrahh," he said.

"I've got some food for you, get down!"

"Raarah."

That was it.

A few nights later he chose a permanent perch on the porch roof next to my bedroom window. I could see him asleep under the stars and the moon. Sometimes I went out in the deepest part of the night and sat on the steps just to be closer to him. He was small and exposed under a huge sky.

In the wild, Chac would now be with a band of teen-age ravens, sweeping into fields, flapping over woods, probing for delicacies along the shore. He was a social animal. But here he had an odd assortment of companions. Once, at dawn, I was watching him through the kitchen window as he stood on the stump I used to split kindling. He had just bathed in the frog pond and was preening and mumbling, but every now and then he stretched his neck out and tilted his head. I stepped closer to the window to see what interested him. It was a young snowshoe hare, less than a foot away, eating grass. I was startled. This, after all, was a full-grown raven, and I would expect a hare to be wary. But it was grazing mildly, and Chac was being pleasantly conversational.

A few days later, Sadie and Chac started a game on the driveway. It began as Sadie walked slowly along. Chac sidled up, all hunched over behind her. He grabbed her tail and gave a sharp yank. She yelped, spun around, and snapped, and he, making his loud, laughing shout, flew up and over and landed in back of her. He pulled her tail again. She spun around, showing her teeth and barking. It looked violent and angry. But when they tired of it, they went their own ways, unhurt and seemingly pleased with themselves.

A pair of sharp-shinned hawks had a nest in the woods close by. One or the other would sometimes fly into the yard to haze Chac, diving and shrieking at him. He would fight back, jumping up, yelling, jabbing at the air. Then the hawk would fly off and Chac would continue walking around, busy with whatever it was that caught his fancy.

Only one thing frightened him. It was the resident raven pair. They flew over the field at least once a day, silent, together, throwing two stern shadows that moved swiftly across the grass. Chac drew in his head and hunched against the ground, stone quiet. It took a while for him to regain his good humor. Why was this?

I read more and found that this pair had actually claimed this land. It was theirs to scavenge in and nest. Chac didn't belong here. If I had taken in a band of young ravens, five or six of them, they would have been able to invade the space and hold it for a time. But one alone did not stand a chance. That might have been why Chac stayed close. My presence, and perhaps Sadie's, offered him some protection. When I walked Sadie on a leash down the road to the bay, he flew close beside us. At the rocks, he examined crabs and mussels and any bright detritus the tide brought us. But above us coasted the dark, disapproving forms.

It was deep summer. One night when there was a full moon and no wind, a scream tore out of Chac. I ran downstairs, flung open the door, and looked up at the porch roof. He was gone.

The next day I walked through the woods with Sadie, calling. There was no answer. I didn't know what had happened to him. Maybe he had been frightened by an owl, or a fisher, or maybe just a coyote trotting too close to the house. Maybe he was not dead.

Ravens are diurnal. They sleep at night. For him to take off in the dark meant that something had terrified him.

The next day my son returned for a break from his job. We walked to the beach on Newbury Neck and took a long swim. We made dinner. In the morning he left, and as I stood in the driveway, waving good-bye, I heard a raven shout. Chac flew down and landed in front of me. He was alive. He had broken through the raven pair's boundary to come home. I rewarded him with his favorite treat: a raw egg, into which he poked a careful hole and sipped the contents.

Then he and Sadie played their game on the driveway.

Once upon a time there was a raven who was neither wild nor tame. There was a dog. There was a woman. One day, in this span of enchantment, the dog and the woman walked down the old woods trail at the back of her house and the raven flew ahead of them just above the trees.

When they reached a stream, the dog and the woman jumped across it and stepped out onto the salt marsh. It was early fall. The grasses were copper-colored and a wind stirred them. The dog rushed ahead. The raven followed just above, flapping and shouting at the top of his voice.

The woman, walking behind them, felt a sudden ache. She wanted more. More days like this. More time together.

But the raven and the dog were not thinking about tomorrow. Tomorrow meant nothing to them. They delighted in this rush down the autumn marsh, one on the ground, the other skimming above in the air. They loved what they had. What they had was now.

Part Two

A Point of View

When he was a young man, Jack Dudley killed one animal at Pocomoonshine Lake he didn't eat. It was a snapping turtle, a female poised on a gravel bank dropping her white, round wet eggs into the hole she had just finished digging. Jack had heard that turtle hearts are ancient motors that pump even when there is no blood flow left. But he wanted to see for himself. He waited as the turtle scraped a cover over the eggs. When she turned back to the lake, he put his boot on her, pinned her, and took her head off with his hunting knife. She walked a few steps before her front legs buckled and the trauma loosened some last drops of fluid that dribbled between her back legs.

She was the color of old sunken logs except for the place where the sudden red blood was spilling. Jack tripped her then, knelt down and cut the carapace from the plastron, opened her up like a sandwich and fetched out the heart. It was beating as he carried it in his hands up to the house his father had built on the shore. He slipped it into a canning jar and filled the jar with water. After watching the heart for a while, he drove over to a doctor's house with the jar and they watched it together. The heart, he told me, roiled the water for an entire day. That was nearly seventy years ago.

A small, compact man, witty, with dry humor and an economy of speech, except when he was in an expansive storytelling mood, Jack had been a lawyer and a judge all his life. He never left the lake he loved for long. When he retired, he brought his second wife, Jane, to the house he grew up in on the southeast shore, on the settlement side. A gravel road goes by it to a few hunting camps. The view from the house looks north onto the long length of water.

When he was in his twenties and away at school, Jack would come home to this house and take a canoe out at night. He pushed it from the shore and paddled off into the dark. He would lie down on its smooth, varnished wooden ribs and go to sleep, drifting and rocking until daybreak, like a child in a cradle. I try to imagine trusting water as big as this to hold you.

Each fall, Jack climbed up onto the roof of his house and swept off the accumulated pine spiles that fell from the century-old trees standing in the yard. And each fall he turned in his loon count. He was the state's only loon-counting participant who refused to report where the nests were located. He knew the good sites, what part of marsh bank and heath cover the birds preferred, and, as the summer wore on, how many chicks had hatched, but he would send in only one number: the young that had survived into September. Loons are secretive at their nests, and Jack figured they had good reason to keep it that way. From his roof he could pause, lean against his broom, and look out over the water through the limbs of the pines. There wasn't a season here he didn't love.

Pocomoonshine is about three miles across and three

miles long. No one knows how it came by its name. It used to be called Shining Lake, perhaps because the road to it, coming down from Kendall Mountain, turns on the ridge, and from there a person can look across almost the entire lake. On a bright and windy day, it flashes in broad sheets of fractured silver. It hurts the eyes.

A marshy peninsula called the Middle Ground extends toward the lake's center. From directly above it, an eagle's view of it, the shape of the open water must look somewhat like a giant moose print in mud. There are small islands scattered north of the Middle Ground, all but one uninhabited. Years of cutting have cleared out most of the big softwoods along the shore. The lake rests in a hollow of boggy, acidic earth and glacial grit—good for tamaracks, canoe birches, swamp maples, sphagnum, and heath plants such as leatherleaf, sweet gale, and highbush blueberry. It is tough, tangled, hard to walk through.

One sort of dam or another has stood for most of the last two hundred years at the outlet at Crawford Lake, a graceful body of water that debouches into the East Machias River. Crawford, Upper and Lower Mud Lakes, and Pocomoonshine are strung together by winding channels like beads on a necklace. By the time Jack was a boy, the cobbled shores and see-through water of a truly wild lake had long disappeared. Water was held back at Crawford by log-driving dams built to collect the wood cut from the forests and to keep the logs afloat as spring meltwater rose. When the dam was thrown open, the cold, tannic-colored water roared into the mouth of the river, tossing the logs in one great pitch toward the mills at East Machias.

After the logging days, a hydroelectric dam was built in the same place. These dams kept the lakes high, holding back water that rose into marshes, loosening and drawing off silt. Eventually the lakes darkened and warmed. Native trout do not thrive without cool pools to rest in and immaculate, see-through water in which to feed. By the time Jack was learning to deep troll with live bait, only an occasional togue rose like a dream of the past out of a last pool in Pocomoonshine. Jack knew, of course, that he had been born to a shore where an essential part of pure wilderness was gone. I think that made him love the wild that was left more fiercely.

Before Jack and his neighbors built the rolling dam at Crawford in the '30s, the lakes had been left open for a few seasons, but the water in them refused to clear. In that time smallmouth bass migrated up the East Machias River, according to old timers who said they watched it happen, and the fish invaded the lakes, establishing a population in Pocomoonshine—the last lake on the chain. The rolling dam was an attempt to halt the movement of new fish species into the lakes, but in the 1980s someone introduced largemouth bass to Pokey, probably slipping young fry out of a bucket into the water, and the lake's transformation was complete: a muddy-bottomed, warm-water, bass-fishing lake.

Jack was one of the first people I knew who lived a sense of place. Pocomoonshine Lake, in Washington County, was his great adventure, wild enough and big enough to use up a lifetime. I met him toward the end of his life, when I had been reading about birds and mammals and plants and was looking for a place where I could go to teach myself what I was trying to learn: to sit still, to wait for something to happen around me, to get myself in an even state of mind so that everything and nothing were equally acceptable. It was also a time toward the end of my marriage.

I drove inland, stayed at a tiny camp, and paddled its coves. Taking my kayak, I headed out into the big stretch of water. Slowly I began to learn something about the lake and about how one man loved it and gave his best attention to it. An apprentice of sorts, I thought the way to live was to learn about Jack's lake. What he was really teaching me was how to settle in wherever I chose to live.

As I got to know Jack and his wife Jane, they offered me the use of the cabin he had built on a narrow peninsula a half a mile or so down-lake from their house and the cabin where I had stayed. There was no road to it. I kayaked across. I remember being alone for five days without hearing another human voice. That had never happened to me before. Time started to wrinkle the way heat does when it rises off a hot tar road in summer. I lost track of it, and it didn't seem to matter.

At Jack's cabin I discovered a deeper aspect of the child I had been, building who I was back to who she was—a person, even then, needing time alone in what was left of wildness, homesick for the sort of experience that people shared with land years ago when there seemed to be a promise of a future unlike the one we have arrived at. I began to trust the instincts of that long-ago child.

Once I woke at night to a thunderstorm. The floor of the cabin shook at each lightning strike. Jagged bolts ripped through the thick and steamy air and the lake water flashed and went dark, flashed and went dark. The smell of sulfur hung in the air. The storm lasted a long time, with periods of engulfing rain. Gradually, it went away. I could look from the window and see it walking across the sky, shaggy, throwing lightning bolts. The lake lay quiet and spent. I sat on the drenched, warm rocks on the shore in my nightgown.

The next evening, when the sky was clear and the lake was calm, I kayaked to the mainland for a visit with Jack and Jane. Jack showed me a silver-framed picture of his father holding him up as a baby, his father's boots in lake water, so that he might take a good look down the length of Pocomoonshine. The baby is dressed in white lace and button-up leather shoes. He squints into the sunshine reflected off the water. As I kayaked back to the cabin at dusk, I turned over in my mind the idea of whether a person can imprint on a place the way a hatchling duckling takes a good look at the face of its mother as it struggles out of the shell, and then will follow her anywhere. You get the picture of the face, or in Jack's case, the lake, and it creates a standard of comfort by which you measure whatever else is real in the world and whatever else is beautiful.

One early morning I worked my kayak toward the channel that leads to Upper Mud Lake. Before I got close to its high rush and sedge borders, I saw two moose standing in deep water up to their withers, lifting their heads, then bending them under the surface and almost disappearing before they came up again, chewing. My kayak was pointed at them. I started to veer away, out into the center of the lake. But the sun caught my paddles and they flashed at the moose like semaphores. The two animals turned slowly, heavily, through the water toward the shore, and the great shoulders of the bull surged upward, sheets of water peeling off him. He waited for the cow to get her footing on the gravel edge—astonishing, I thought, his apparent courtesy—and when she did, his hooves hit the rocks behind her, sharp, like rifle shots, and they were gone behind the trees.

In the last year of his life, from his daybed window, Jack watched the November ice set. When I phoned, which I did often, he told me that the ice would start at the shore, not thick enough for a man to walk on or a loon to hunch up on, but every morning when he looked out, it had extended itself during the night, and every noon, it melted back some. But when dark fell, it began reaching out in points again, smoothing the water, quieting it. Jack was seventy-eight. His heart was giving out. He had trouble walking.

I got off the phone and wondered how many times he put his hand to that stuttering canter in his chest and thought back to the heart in the jar. As he recalled parts of his life for the last time, he told me without a trace of irony the story of the snapper's heart. He liked remembering the fuss it made: a Permian muscle so much tougher than his own.

For me, Jack had become the lake and everything in it. I would think about him there at the shore, stretched out on the daybed by the window looking at the water, and my mind would go from him to the eagle I had seen standing on a beaver lodge near Big Mud, or a translucent mayfly hatch I had kayaked through, the iridescent wings in the evening light creating a nimbus around my kayak. My mind would go to an old snapping turtle I had watched paddling underwater, its neck stretched out, poking its beaked snout into hollows between sunken logs, hunting for fish or frogs or insect larvae, its carapace covered in a waving coat of brown algae. It was a grand old man carrying an underwater map in its head, a quick-striking curmudgeon disguised in lake duff.

Jack was worried about a young loon that had hatched late. It was not large enough or old enough to fly. Every day a parent skimmed down lifting furls of water. It fussed around the chick. It was flying in from the St. Croix River, about seven miles away. In a few weeks, the adult birds and their young would be moving down the river and into Passamaquoddy Bay, thirty miles to the coast. Jack said that he heard the parent before it set down. When it was only a dot in the sky, it would call out and the chick would spin around to face the sound. A loon needs an eighth of a mile of free water for takeoff.

Ice soon prevented that. Once or twice Jack saw a parent fly over when it could no longer come down. He watched the ice close the young bird in. The days passed. The young loon circled in its small, dark bath. One morning the open water was gone. And so was the chick. And fall was over at last.

Three weeks after Jack died, I returned to Pocomoonshine. I told no one I was coming. I stopped my car at Kendall Mountain, opened the door, and got out and looked down, seeing the lake for the first time in winter, frozen beneath a haze of cold air, the trees around it, rimed. Then I drove to the boat dock and walked across the lake ice to the Middle Ground. My life was taking me elsewhere, and I had come back to Pocomoonshine to get a last look. I knew by then that Jack had been, for me, one of those great people who enter another person's life, and just by being themselves, change the way that person lives in the world.

At the Middle Ground I found a cedar stump. I sat down and faced the opposite shore, searching for that one-room cabin. It took me a while before my eyes made out the roofline hidden behind the red pines. I couldn't see the window where I once stood and watched the lightning flash. At this distance the little cabin was no more or less than a tree or a rock ledge, a part of the lake's topography.

A coyote's track cut into the snow by the stump where I sat. It was a crusted old trail. I imagined the animal, its fur thick against the cold, its tail straight and flared. In my mind I saw the coyote pause to sniff this stump on a night when a first-quarter moon shone down. The coyote was hungry and had caught the scent of vole. Then it started up the solid lake and was joined by two more coyotes, and they trotted nearly the length of it. The lake, I imagined, was moon-white in color. It was noisy, booming and contracting with sounds like rifle shots. For a time the coyotes continued along the center of the lake, casting pale shadows. They passed in front of the cabin, made a right angle into the trees, and were gone. Now the lake was empty again. Nothing moved except the straining increments of ice. But many things were possible: a moose might step out from a thicket or a fox might follow in the footprints of the coyotes for a yard or two. The flight of a great horned owl might cast a quick shadow.

If a person were here to listen she might catch the sound of a vole skittering into its snow tunnel above solid ice and the water, above the bottom mud of the lake where an old snapper sleeps away the cold.

The Gift

It was in early October, with the leaves falling off the red maples and drifting into the yard, that I first noticed my house was crammed with the past. Like a trap it held me to what was already gone. Two years after my divorce, and now I could see this. And I could see ahead.

My children were off at college. I shut the doors to the rooms with their beloved childhood things. Those rooms were for them to come home to. Everything else, I started to throw away. The marital bed. The busted couch. The TV that got one station—sometimes. Cracked plates, badly fixed chairs, broken tables, old clothes, old magazines. I rented a neighbor's truck, and the man who managed the dump got to know me. He waved me through as I drove in with load after load, climbed up on the truck bed, and tossed stuff. Broken tools, broken radios, buckets with holes in them, faded postcards, bald tires, cooking pots with no handles, warped thirty-threes, splintered picture frames.

"Here again, I see," he said one day, his tone less friendly than before. No one he knew threw away everything. "Are you sure this all comes from one place?"

"Positive," I told him. Work boots without heels, sprung toasters, split chains for vanished chainsaws, a lawnmower missing a blade, a wheelbarrow without a wheel. By the time I finished, the house and the shed were nearly bare and it was a new season—winter. I kept the few things I needed, nothing else. I walked around this brand-new space as light poured into the scrubbed emptiness.

A man I cared for took a break from work and came to stay for a time. He was a field biologist. He brought with him a large dead calf. A farmer had given him a call after the calf died in the barn. He thought a biologist might be able to use the body, and my friend had lifted it into the back of his truck.

"Maybe it will attract something," he said, and dragged it over the crusted snow to the brush pile before the trees. He took out his camp knife, slit it from throat to crotch, opened it up, and tied it by its neck to a stump with a thick piece of rope.

Even from the kitchen window the calf was a shock on the snow. Its lungs were scarlet and frothy. Its heart was a pink stone. Its multicolored iridescent guts were spun with veins, and its fat was creamy, and, of course, frozen hard. It lay innocently, indecently spread-eagle in the serious cold, tethered by the rope. I put on my coat that first night and walked out and stood by it for a while, as if it needed tending.

In the morning we stood at the window and gazed at the calf. Nothing had touched it. We snowshoed over the crust around the bay and in the afternoon we baked bread, and after a few days, he left to go back to his job, and I went up to my study to write.

Still nothing had touched the calf.

But one night, taking Sadie out for a last walk before bedtime, I heard a shuffle on the snow over where the calf's body lay. The next morning, when the dark had receded enough to see shapes, I stood at the bedroom window and watched two coyotes pulling at the frozen guts. One was light gray, so pale I might have called it white. The other was red. It was especially cold outside, and their coats stood up. They looked enormous, like wolves. Every now and then they would take a long look at the house as the light came in through the trees and the sun rose over the east hill.

The day passed, dark fell, and coyotes howled beside the body. The following day the two coyotes were there again. They were fearless. They ripped up and gulped down as much as they could get before the sun went down. I suspected then that the nighttime howlers were not the same animals as these two in broad daylight. This was a hefty calf, and there was a lot of it to eat. Its head with the frozen milk-colored eyes was huge. Its legs and ribs and haunches were thick. This eating business, I began to think, might go on for a while. And for a while I would have coyotes day and night in my yard.

I opened the kitchen door and brought Sadie out on the snow with a leash snapped to her collar. The two coyotes looked up from the calf and watched her, then went back to gnawing.

But the next day the calf was gone. Femurs, ribs, skull, backbone, hips, shoulders, tail, pelvis, hooves, and every trace of blood and flesh were gone. Only a shed of hairs marked the place where it had rested. And the empty noose.

I phoned a neighbor.

He came over, and we followed the coyote trail, noting where it crossed the deer path. It went down into a gully where a half-frozen stream gurgled energetically, then up onto a ridge. One would never guess the coyotes were carrying away sections of gnawed calf. Not a bit seemed to have touched the snow. When we had followed the tracks quite far, when we had exited our territory and seemed, eerily, to have entered theirs, without more than a few words between us, we turned around and came back. And that was all.

The moon and the stars shone into the windows of my house that night. I turned off the lights and stood in the phosphorescent shimmer from the sky. More than halfway through my life, I had come to a place that was my own. When the sun rose again, the snow was clean—all traces of pain and loss, hunger and blood, were gone.

Alewives

An alewife is a beautiful fish. Its back is dark blue, its belly, silver. It is laterally compressed, deep from dorsal fin to the sharp belly scales that can slice the skin on the palm of your hand, and as narrow from gill to gill as a pack of cards, a perfect shape to move up down-rushing water. Put your hand in a fast stream, your fingers pointed into the current, and feel the water part. You can't do it with your palm catching the flow, but it is easy when you aim your fingers upstream, the way an alewife aims its snout.

In the 1970s and for generations before that, Patten

Stream, in my town, supported one of the best commercial alewife runs in the state. In the old days, alewives grew to be over a foot long. They could weigh up to a pound. But today, if we see them at all, they are younger, smaller fish. They were sold to lobster cooperatives for trap bait, to companies that made fish meal, and to people who hung them in their smokehouses and made a tough pemmican for the general stores along the coast. As a child, my son loved to eat the smoked alewives that used to be stacked on the counters of every store. They were soft-boned, darkly fleshed, sweetly chewy. They tasted of salt and a hint of mold.

Alewives still gather at Patten Bay at the mouth of Patten Stream in the spring. When the ice lets go and the rains come, you can hear the stream as you drive over it on Route 172. It sounds like half a dozen people standing inside the culvert under the road practicing their kettledrums. White plumes of water pitch over boulders. Patten Stream is beautiful this time of year because it cannot contain such excess.

Over fifty years ago, Wayne McGraw's father bought a lease from the town to harvest alewives. He built a wooden footbridge above the mouth of the stream, just before the bay, and when his boys were tall enough, he taught them to lean out over the bridge and scoop up the fish in dip nets, just as Wayne taught his own sons when they were grown.

"The year before the run dropped off for good, we had the biggest catch ever," he told me. "They came into Patten Bay so thick the bay was solid. It looked like you could walk across on their backs. And I think there might have been almost as many seals out there. And the gulls were screaming so loud you couldn't hear yourself think. Anyone who hasn't seen it can't imagine it: a path of fish stretching clear down this bay."

"But they just stopped coming like they used to. For fifty years I saw them swim in by the thousands. Some years we'd land twenty-four thousand bushels, maybe more, and every spring they'd be back."

People in town used to time their lives to seasonal events such as the alewife run. Today, most of us hardly notice when it comes. The loss of a huge number of fish has changed the bay, the stream, and the ponds where they once spawned, where their eggs and fry fed other species of freshwater fish. And it has changed the people who live here. The alewife runs all along the coast dropped off at about the same time. Overfishing, dams, the heating up of the breeding ponds as a result of those dams and other impediments, pollution runoff: these trespasses contributed to the bust. But there is something more, something we can't quite read.

Here in Surry, there is no trace left of the old footbridge. Route 172 crosses the stream, and when the road was last upgraded, a big new culvert was laid down to usher the water underneath and deposit it back in its bed fifty yards before the bay. The culvert sits on a riprap of boulders, and sometimes, when the spring melt and the rains are not ample, it stands above the streambed and spews out a thin ribbon of water. It is a hung culvert. The alewives coming in from the ocean cannot reach it.

One spring, a group of neighbors and I and our children climbed down the bank with nets and five-gallon buckets and caught alewives trapped in the pools and thrashing at the lip of the culvert. We hauled them up and across the road and released them back into the stream. We worked in a haze of sweat and blackflies, but still, when we left, there were hundreds of fish schooling below.

When I drove by Patten Stream this spring, I spotted an osprey and four gulls wheeling over the maples and birches that grow along the banks. They were dropping down toward the charging water where it meets the bay. I got a quick look at the blunt heads of two seals out in the high tide, and I knew the time had come. The alewives were back.

The rains had been good and Patten was a wild and muscular surge of water. Above it, the branches of the trees crisscrossed the air with their pale unfolding leaves. I turned my car around and headed back, drove down the dirt road to the town landing, and pulled to a stop. A telephone lineman had parked his yellow truck next to the stream. He was eating a sandwich, sitting in the truck with the door open and watching the scene, in spite of the light rain.

I got out of my car for a closer look. Rain squalled across the bay. The backs of the fish pierced the surface, hugging the mouth of the stream. Three ospreys circled down and rose again as the fish sank beneath their shadows. Herring and black-backed gulls stood on the rocks screaming.

I sat down on a rock across from them. In front of me five cormorants were swiveling and diving through the fish. Cormorants have eyes with bright turquoise irises. From where I sat, I could see the color. I could see the orange gular pouches, the slack skin at their throats. One bird dove, came up wrestling a silver-bellied fish, flipped it into the air, caught it face-first, and swallowed. The two harbor seals hung in the water, their huge, black eyes keyed to the stream. No one seemed to notice me, not even the great blue heron stepping elegantly along the opposite bank as the stream foamed and pitched across the rocks and shot straight into the tide. One by one, some of the fish slipped up to rest in the dark pools by the sides of the rocks before they tried the next step.

"Nobody owns anyone, except in memory," John Updike wrote. I suppose that goes for owning wild migratory fish in a hometown stream as well. We can spend our lives regretful. We can watch three ospreys and want a dozen. We can hear the shattering screams of twenty gulls and know that a true cacophony is a hundred of them, each one insisting on its own insatiable hunger. We can want fish we can walk over, but those are Wayne McGraw's memories, not ours. I would like to see what he saw, but I don't dare miss what is here now. I was taking it all in, just like the lineman, loving the rain, these hungry birds and seals, these silver-bellied, blue-backed fish, maybe a couple of thousand of them, rushing for the deep pockets between the rocks. They will spawn in Upper and Lower Patten ponds this year, then swim back down. Before fall settles in, their young will ride the current to the bay. The water will get them there and back for now.

The lineman stepped out of his truck and squatted on a rock next to me. Together we watched the fish leap and slide and hammer their way up.

The pitching water was so loud we couldn't have heard each other speak even if we had wanted to. The fish, one by one, hurdled, fell back, hurdled, fell back. Then one kinked its way into a higher pool. The lineman and I saw it resting there, slowly sweeping its tail back and forth, and we turned to each other and grinned.

The Alder Patch

The small, dark thing on the road was a snowshoe hare, a kit, no more than six or seven inches long. It was hopping across the hardtop like a piece of balled-up paper pushed erratically by the wind. I stopped the car. Heedless of my presence, it hopped a few yards in front of my tires.

It had come out of the alders that run in a wide swath at a right angle to the road along the east side of a blueberry field. The alder patch is about five acres, punctuated by feral apple trees, a few tamaracks, a few white pines. It is a rich, impenetrable tangle where birds nest and does give birth to fawns. In this case, a snowshoe hare, only a little more than a week ago, had produced young somewhere in its protection, in what is called a "form," a shallow, hidden depression. Not a rabbit hole. New World rabbits and hares do not dig holes or live in community warrens.

Snowshoe kits are born with their eyes open, and in a few days they are hopping. This one was probably already nibbling plants, sampling the various tastes and textures, although it should have been under the dam's protection still, and its rudderless skitter across the road seemed odd. Charming, but odd. I turned off the motor, waiting to see its mother. Or perhaps a second kit.

Instead, a bobcat jumped onto the road's shoulder, its eyes keyed to the hare. It never looked in my direction, never seemed to notice the car. Like a hugely oversized housecat, it trotted after the little hare in that tense, clenched manner of hunting cats.

"Stop right there!" I shouted, throwing the car door open. What was I doing? I had no idea. I wagged my finger at the bobcat. It looked startled—what was this?—but held its ground.

"Don't even think about it!" I said.

I knew if the bobcat did not eat this little hare it would find someone else. But I was here, not somewhere else, and the hare was making an especially poor job of escape.

The bobcat sat down in the middle of the road as I rushed past it after the tiny ball of gray-brown fluff that scooted under a thatch of grass on the other side. Reaching my hand into the grass, I touched its fur. It screamed—that horrible cry that hares make at the point of grave injury and impending death that cancels out all the muteness of their former lives. Instinctively, I drew back. The cat jumped forward. For perhaps less than a second we both rummaged in the grass as the hare filled our ears with its grating terror.

My hand closed over its soft fur. I lifted the hare and stuck it under my sweater. The screaming stopped. The cat leaped over the shoulder and sat down beside an ant-hill under a pine and stared at me. It was a tall, vertical cat with black tufts on the tips of its ears, a puggish face, huge flecked golden eyes set close together, and a stump for a tail.

We stared at one another. The cat showed no real fear, but rather a sort of bemused caution, a hesitation, as if it had met with something puzzling that had stolen its lunch, as if things might right themselves, and the hare—mysteriously gone—might reappear. But I turned around, with the tiny life quiet against my belly, got back into the car, and drove home.

In the kitchen I stood holding this almost weightless creature up to the window light. Through its loose skin, I could feel its bones. Its black eyes seemed, somehow, far away, unfocused. What was I doing with this animal in my hands? I had been a wild bird rehabilitator for years, and people had brought me young mammals they had found, no matter that my license was only for birds. The little hares always died. I never saved a one.

Folding the hare under my sweater again, I telephoned a friend, a wild animal rehabilitator. I told her the story.

"Uh-huh," she said. I had hoped for a bit more.

"I have no idea why I did this," I explained, suddenly embarrassed. "Now I'm stuck."

"You're not really," she said. "Just put it back."

"Of course. That's what I'll do," I agreed. How many times had I told people to reach up and set nestlings back in their nests? That most birds have no sense of smell, that parents will take their babies back. But it is riskier with mammals, whose sense of smell is primary.

Hanging up the phone, I held the creature to the light again. I could see red veins through the pink flesh of its ears. The soft nose drew air in and out. The black lashes of its shiny blank eyes, the shock white blaze of fur between the ears, the weightless weight of it—everything was beautiful, this particular life, in this particular moment of light pouring in from the window.

Put it back. The only thing.

I walked down the road carrying the hare under my sweater. We entered the alder patch, not an easy task. We followed a deer trail for a few yards, then turned off into a dense mat of ferns and Canada mayflowers. Kneeling, I broke off some of the fern fronds and rubbed their fresh green scent against its body, erasing, I hoped, any scent of me. And then I opened my hands.

Its silken body slipped from between my fingers. It ran away wholeheartedly.

I sat, listening for any sound, ready to protect the sprinter who, I assumed, was seeking its dam. Somewhere close by, a white-throated sparrow tried half a song and gave up. The leafy crosshatch of alder branches stretched around me up to the sky, and at my feet the ferns overlapped. I was deep in a wild green nest. No one walking by or driving on the road would guess I was here.

The earth smelled damp and sweet in the alders. I could hear, at a distance, terns crying above the incoming tide, and across the road down at the salt marsh, crow-shriek. Maybe the crows had discovered a barred owl perched for the day and were trying to rout it. Maybe they had come upon the nesting goshawks. Maybe the bobcat was crossing the salt grass, nosing into the tunnels of voles, its sudden appearance upsetting the crows.

The day was warm. I closed my eyes and settled in. A yellowthroat sang nearby. It occurred to me, rather drowsily, that I had never seen a bobcat here before.

This is my neighborhood of millions of lives, depending on how and whom you count. From springtails to moose, from June bugs to people, from boreal shrimp to harbor porpoises, it is a small, green place by water. It is a tiny irreplaceable place where we go about the everyday magic of our lives.

Country Road

The first time I saw the Cross Road, it was a dirt road that led to the bay. My husband drove our secondhand Chevrolet wagon down it, and a swirl of dust lifted behind us. We stopped at the water. My children leaned out the windows to take a good look. The waste blueberry fields on either side shone coppery in the late October sun. The bay smelled of brine and seaweed. It lay before us, shallow as a pie plate, with granite stones—the old glacial erratics—sitting deep in the low-tide mud, casting their shadows east.

We moved from our cabin in Gouldsboro and built a

house on a nine-acre woodlot off this road, a quarter of a mile from the bay. The road, the bay, the fields, woods, and two salt marshes seemed a place within a place, a secret tucked away in a tucked-away town. Red maples and white pines and red oaks that grew on either side of the road reached their branches across as if to touch each other with their tips. They looked something like those tea-colored nineteenth-century photographs of New England villages where American elms before the blight arched above streets creating a canopy through which one could walk to scenes they framed beyond. Under the limbs of our trees, we caught a tiny triangular glint of the bay at high tide.

Our children walked the hill to piano lessons and rode their bikes to the bay beneath this moving filigree of light and shadow, and sometimes, on the way, they discovered a ruffed grouse taking a dust bath in high summer, or, after a hard rain, when the dirt was pocked with puddles, they found young green frogs resting in the muddy water.

The Cross Road wasn't just any road. It was specific and original, and it sank its wonderful variety into their growing lives. That it was unique, a throwback road, they barely noticed. But they did know that in winter it was one of the last roads plowed. It could stop a school bus and grant its own particular snow day. My children and I skied it then. And if the moon was full, we went at night, carrying our skis and poles up to the cemetery where our Union soldiers lie, and coasted past them all the way down to the frozen bay.

The Cross Road would still be a dirt road if it were not for progress. It might have become an example, eventually, of what it looks like to nourish the present by preserving the best of the past. Maybe our children would have told their children that this old road with its dust and spring heaves and mud puddles proves that people, who are good at improving things, can be just as good at knowing when to leave things alone.

"You've got to go with the future, with progress. You know that," a selectman told me when I phoned him to find out if the rumor was true, if the town was planning to pave the Cross Road.

"What is progress?" I asked. He ignored this. It wasn't really a question.

Developments were going up on the east side of the bay, with saltwater views and expensive vacation homes, and each new house was a plush cushion of taxes for the town. Before the roads and the houses were built, the Cross Road had been patched with tar at the top of the hill where it turned off Route 176. Every few summers, a layer of hot macadam was smacked onto it and rolled flat, and the ditches on either side were scooped out by men with shovels on a work crew. Every other spring the rains washed away the summer's work. The road had a stubborn, bony streak.

This could have gone on forever, this back and forth between men and the seasons, if the drivers of the gravel, lumber, loam, and fill trucks had not chosen to turn down the Cross Road because it was a short cut to the developments. The trucks bore down day after day. Their drivers, men whose faces we could not discern through the windshields and who didn't seem to notice us at the sides of the road, were in a hurry. Their speed and the weight of their trucks created washboards and washouts and deep potholes. They stirred up serious dust storms that coated the trees in a fine power until the next hard rain.

Our longest-serving selectman enjoyed an active tenure in this town. He also owned a shoreline of woods and beach sand, a place on Toddy Pond that he could have sold to a developer, as so many others were doing, and pocket a small fortune. But he had not done this. What is more, he allowed a few people to swim there in summer, and I was one of them.

After work, I would call my dog, William, into the car, and we would drive to the pond. No one else was around. We stepped onto the trail leading through the woods, and it is hard to say who loved these evenings best. When he got to the beach, William trotted to the rocky point, serious about otter smell, dead sunfish, a painted turtle's tracks. Finished with inventory, he plopped down in the warm slosh as I swam out and floated on my back. No one else was ever here except for a loon or two bobbing in deep water. The only sounds were the water's even chuck and sometimes a call from one of the birds.

This particular selectman was also our town commissioner of roads. He worked for the Maine Department of Transportation. Roads were his business, perhaps even his passion, and the Cross Road's washboards and mud holes, its gullies and rocks, vexed his sense of order. When I called him, he agreed to walk the road with a few of us who live here.

"We'll be taking no more than two or three yards on either side—and that means, of course, cutting these trees," he explained as we went. "I suppose we can try to get away with less here, and maybe over there. The new road will mostly work against these little rises, and the dips you have now. It'll be pretty much a straight grade to the cemetery."

Distracted by the song of a veery, my neighbor Hugh turned away to listen to the full-throated music coming through the trees: a bar of downward-slanting, burry notes that ended and at once started back at the top and rolled down again. A rhapsody of musical hills and valleys, of rises and dips. The song stopped him in his tracks.

"I think," Hugh said, "we should be protecting trees,

not trucks." With that, he reached out and took hold of an old pine. He fit his arms around it, rested the side of his face against it, and hugged it. The rest of us stared.

Then I laughed at the theater of the gesture. I couldn't help it. We all knew we didn't stand a chance of changing the selectman's mind or the town's plans. If we had thought we needed to protect this road of ours, we would have begun the work to save it years before it was in any danger. Why not hug a doomed tree now?

A quick smile played across the selectman's face, and soon the walk ended.

In the next few months, we listened to the felling of trees, the blasting of bedrock, the trucking in and trucking out, the building up and smoothing down. And the paving over. Every day, except on weekends, we could hear just what part of the road we were losing. When it was done, it was smooth, with perfectly even shoulders and ditches and culverts to carry away rainwater.

The selectman saved the tree that Hugh had hugged. There it stood in all its shaggy out-of-place majesty, leaning over the brand-new surface. He had given it—and us—a tip of his hat.

In this time of transformation, I learned what is worth saving. Beauty is worth saving. An impractical, beautiful dirt road with a shading canopy can nourish a person's mind and spirit, and people who are fed by the lovely aspects around them enrich the life of any town.

Letting Summer Go

Here, in the most northeasterly part of the country, I dropped my fear of snakes. I could pick up any snake I found, and did, and if by chance one bit me—if I handled it carelessly—a bite was all I got. In Maine there are no poisonous snakes left. We can live with snakes without prejudice. The primal fear of snakes that once saved human lives is not necessary here.

Before the hard frost, when night temperatures drop but the days heat up, and light in the hardwood trees looks burnished as if it had passed through a glass of hard cider, snakes bask on the road at the end of my driveway. The pavement is a smooth outcrop radiating the last warmth of summer. The noon sun beats down on their backs, and their bellies take in the stored heat of the road that cuts through woods and the few small fields like an ancient seam of basalt, a smooth extrusion.

But, of course, the road is not an outcrop, and cars come along and kill the snakes. I have found them, their spines and fine ribs exposed, their jaws smashed. I pick them up, and so do my neighbors, and we set them down on the shoulder for a raven or a skunk, a fisher or a fox to eat.

A week ago, I found a young garter snake stretched out on the road like a chunk of clothesline, alive. It was about a foot long. I thought at first that the tip of its tail had been run over. But when I picked it up, I saw that something wet and pink hung from its vent. Garter snakes will sometimes lunge and bite when they are handled, but this one did not. They sometimes let go drops of musk from glands at the base of the tail, cool to the touch, smelling sweet and rotten. This garter did not. It had dark pebbled scales highlighted in yellow stripes, one stripe on either side and one along its back.

I was on my way to the bay to see if the winter ducks had flown in yet. I stuffed the injured snake into the chest pocket of my fleece jacket, zipped it up, and felt the animal settle at my right breast. The wind was blowing. The mid-tide water sloshed against the rocks. I walked the head of the bay, past feral apple trees where bright red apples hung, and where fresh deer tracks pocked the ground. There were no ducks out on the water. Three loons, two parents and a grown chick, floated close to shore.

This time of year, I, too, search for the last warm corners, for the sheltered haunts where the sun is hot and where summer seems to linger. But in truth, it has already gone: the bumblebees and the flowers they threw themselves into are dead; most of the warblers have left, except for a few yellow-rumps picking at spider egg sacks that hang from shed rafters. The phoebes are gone, and so are the dragonflies. All but one of the kingfishers have deserted the bay, and any day now, the winter ducks will be back.

In a dusty old book of country stories I took out from the library, I read that a farmer killed what he thought was the last timber rattler in Maine. He dragged the body home and nailed it by its rattle, head down, to his barn door. The next day he found another rattlesnake curled beneath it. The second snake must have tracked the scent of the dragged body. The farmer killed that one, too—and this time he probably did get the last Maine rattler—but a snake following another snake unsettled him. It implied constancy and perhaps even affection. The possibility that the last Maine rattlers might have cared for each other, like two refugees living hidden in the forest, was a concept that could make even a hard-bitten farmer feel a little bit like a murderer.

I found a discarded soup pot for the garter snake to live in, and picked up my reptile book. Following its directions, I spread two layers of paper towels in the bottom of the pot, added dirt, a small capful of water, and made what seemed to me a pleasing landscape of leaves and pebbles with one smooth sunning rock. From the compost pile I dug up earthworms for the snake to eat. My study is a small room on the second floor of the house. Setting the pot on top of a bookshelf where the snake could enjoy a full stream of light from the window, I sat down to my work.

Writing is a silent endeavor, and so is the life of a snake. In that bright room, we were well-suited companions. The next few days the weather outside grew colder, warmed, then grew cold again. But we hardly noticed. In its diminutive Eden, the snake seemed to busy itself. If I listened carefully, I could hear it move over the leaves. When I looked in, I saw its clean beauty, its head like a highly polished button, and the flick of its splayed black tongue. The injury healed in four days until only a crust hung from its vent. I cut it off with a pair of kitchen scissors, and began to entertain the thought that I might keep the snake through the winter. This creature in my study would be my gesture against time, a flag holding fast to the dream of a summer country full of sunlight, the high tide in the bay warm enough to swim in, the nights smelling of earth, the nesting birds feeding their young.

Snakes that hibernate live longer than those that do not, if you count by years. If you count heartbeats, it is about the same. By reducing the number of beats, a snake in hibernation rations its supply. But how do we measure the quality of time, the months spent asleep just below the frost line, the heart ticking now and then like a worn-out clock? Are those months worth a handful of summer days? Surely if this little garter could choose, it would choose summer.

I looked forward to a shedding, the snake cramped and immobile in the leaves, turning a milky blue, the skin splitting and peeling above its eyes. I would witness the gradual emergence of a creature as bright as a restored fresco. Even the sclera of a snake's eyes is shed, and the new vision is immaculate and true.

One morning I walked into the study and looked into the soup pot. It was empty. I glanced around the room, feeling a rise of panic. The snake could be anywhere. In the pile of papers. In the pile of old magazines. Under the rug. Behind the file cabinet. How do you find a snake? I pulled back the rug and shook it. I sorted the papers, restacked the magazines. I yanked the mattress off the bed. No snake.

How long could it live in this house? Would it feed on overwintering spiders and drink water from the leaky bathroom faucet? Would it carry on in secret, moving up and down the stair treads? Walking around the house barefoot in the evening dark, listening to my own feet on the floorboards, I thought about the snake's keeled belly scales. Perhaps, in the still house, they would make a sound as it moved, a dry ticking.

In bed, in the dark, I listened.

Thanksgiving was only five weeks away. My daughter would be home. What if I couldn't find the snake by then? Her aversion to snakes is absolute. What if she were in her room at night, in her bed, reading a book, and turned to a slight stir issuing from her bookcase to see the snake's face emerge between two of her favorite volumes, and then its entire body would slip out and dangle headfirst and drop to the rug? What then?

Drifting in and out of sleep, I revisited the story of a friend of ours who had fought in Vietnam. He came home to Maine peppered with shrapnel, but that meant less to him than the night when he lay somewhere in the jungle, in his sleeping bag, listening to the constant dripping of the leafy jungle trees. He heard something slip through the tent flap and felt whatever it was nudge into his bag. It was a large snake. It moved along his bare arm, then lifted across his body and settled heavily onto his chest. He felt his heart go nuts. He knew he would die. He knew his racketing heart would eventually upset the snake, and that intakes of breath—however small—would annoy it. He closed his eyes. He felt the snake shift and readjust. It lifted its head quickly, then relaxed—a false alarm—and rested it in the curls of his chest hair. Its face was close to his and it seemed for a time to sleep. But he waited for it to strike. He would not be able to move his hands fast enough to protect his throat, his mouth or cheeks, his eyes. He felt his arms fall asleep, tingling at his sides. And then, after what seemed a few hundred years, the snake slipped off his chest and ducked out of the tent.

My daughter still remembers this story.

That is not all she remembers. When she was eight years old, we visited the Okefenokee Swamp in Georgia and were told that a man who called himself Okefenokee Joe would appear on stage at the visitors' center. He would offer insights into snakes.

I hoped that he would loosen some of my daughter's

unnecessary fear. She was growing up around red bellies, greens, ringnecks, garters—the most innocent of snakes—all of them passing their summers discreetly in the rock jumbles and the cleared field, the kitchen garden, and by the frog ponds. I hoped for an avuncular man sitting, perhaps, in an old country rocker, spinning stories about snake virtues. Maybe, eventually, he would draw out of a wicker picnic basket one of those gorgeous orange and yellow Georgia corn snakes and invite the children onto the stage to touch its shiny scales.

We sat down in the front row. The day was hot. The theater at the small center overflowed with tourists like ourselves, northern people, pale and a little ill at ease in shorts and sandals. When the curtain drew back, Okefenokee Joe stood at center stage. He wore tight jeans, a white T-shirt, and high black rubber boots, a big silver buckle gleamed at his belt. His moustache drooped at either side of his mouth.

"Welcome," he told us. He explained that he was wearing the boots because he'd been out in the swamp since dawn hunting up THE BIGGEST RATTLER IN THE STATE OF GEORGIA.

I felt my daughter sink back in her chair. Joe strutted the length of the stage carrying a snake stick that looked somewhat like a golf club, a metal shaft with a perpendicular foot on which a snake can be coaxed to balance itself. Swinging the stick casually as he talked, he detailed the effects of a rattler's poison on the human body compared to the poison of a cottonmouth, the pain of a rattler's bite compared to the soft chomp of a coral snake. He warned us against the cryptic coloring of copperheads, masters of disguise.

"They're good at fooling you," he said.

He offered the further observation that cottonmouths are snakes with curiosity. If one slapped into our canoe from an overhanging branch as we paddled the swamp, the worst thing we could do was to panic. A cottonmouth in your canoe starts off just curious, he said, but if you panic, it might change its attitude. And that wouldn't be for the better, most likely. And there you would be in the canoe, watching its curiosity start to fade, and you with only a paddle to defend yourself, and panicking like crazy, and the alligators, floating nearby with only their eyes and nostrils and the spines of their tails showing, making it impossible to escape by throwing yourself overboard. Not a good scene, as Joe explained it, and one that could be avoided if you kept tight control of your primal fears, which he was exacerbating with every word out of his mouth.

I looked around the room for a way to get my daughter out of there, but the aisles were blocked. What I hadn't had time to pay much attention to was the wooden box at stage left. It had narrow vents along its side. A lock hung from its clasp. A man in a wheelchair sat in the aisle beside me and I observed that his face was slightly flushed and his eyes were keyed to the box. It was no more than ten feet from us. A sound came from within, an autumnal sound: a fluttering of dry beech leaves.

Joe leaned down and undid the lock. "I got us this great big fella right here," he said softly, lifting back the top of the box.

"STAND ASIDE!" he shouted and jumped back. We were packed too tight. We couldn't stand aside. The man in the wheelchair took a quick breath. My daughter grabbed my hand. Nothing happened. We watched Joe circle the box, jabbing at the air above it with his stick. Every time he jabbed, a gust of wind stirred those leaves.

"What's going on in there?" he complained, leaning his face over the box. As if in response, a head rose. It was as big as a human fist, broad and flat, mottled gray in color. Two pale eyes with vertical pupils looked straight at us. Then the head dropped quickly back.

Joe walked around the box again, making a lot of noise with his rubber boots, but the snake, with good reason, wanted nothing to do with him. Bracing the sole of his boot on the side of the box, he upended it. It slapped down on the stage and the snake went sprawling.

An eastern diamondback can grow to six feet or more. This one, struggling on the slick boards, was close. It stopped its flailing and assumed the letter "S." It drew back its head, pointed it at Joe, stuck up the tip of its tail and rattled. Joe poked it with his stick. It struck. It struck again. It missed him both times and decided to escape, heading for the curtains. When that didn't work, it made a dash toward us. Joe—bless him—cut it off.

He teased the rattler around the stage, but the audience was growing restless. We didn't like this. And the day was going by outside. And the snake seemed tired. Maybe even a little depressed.

Sensing he couldn't hold the crowd, Joe pushed his stick beneath the snake's belly. He lifted the stick in both hands with a flourish so that the front half of the snake hung in the air. The rest of it slumped on the stage floor, and the curtains closed.

I grabbed my daughter's hand. Outside she yanked herself away from me and leaned stiffly, almost formally, toward me.

"I don't like snakes," she told me. "As a matter of fact, now I hate them. I will always hate them."

⌄

Deep into the night of the missing snake, a warm air blew from the south. Within that fertile silence, I had drifted back to a place tinged with fear and woke to a morning breeze stirring the curtains. I got up and stepped into the bathroom. There on a Mexican tile, in a beam of early sun, rested the little snake. Its delicate body draped the tile in the letter "S."

I picked it up, walked outside, and found a perfect hibernaculum for it to sleep through the cold—old leaves, rotted timbers, a pile of fieldstones—and I let summer go.

Knowing Things

When my children were very young, after my husband and I had put them to bed, I would sometimes throw a shawl over my shoulders and step outside to stand under the stars. Kerosene lamps lighted our cabin windows, pale, extinguishable flames. The stars were bright and quiet. As I stared up at them, I began to let in the silence of the natural world.

Silence was a huge presence in these woods, and it reached from the cabin to the stars. Sometimes, an owl's call broke it. Or a coyote howled. But always, the silence resumed. It overpowered sound. Standing in the dark, looking up, I imagined myself falling headfirst away from this place as if the gravity that held me here could easily weaken and fail.

But in daylight, the ground held me tight. The rush and tumble of living sounds reassured me and gave my children and me new things to discover. During this time I began to teach myself something about wild birds.

It was as if I had been given a bag of live puzzle parts. No matter how many pieces I figured out how to fit together—this beak shape goes with that wing shape, with those feet and legs—there was more here than my lifetime would allow. As long as my interest held, the questions kept coming, and I kept pulling on my boots and picking up my binoculars and my father's old bird guide to go outside to try to find the answers. This felt like gravity to me.

Once I took the binoculars into the woods to the outlet stream of a nearby pond and sat against a pine. After a time, a black bird splashed into the water in front of me. It began diving. I reported to my family I had seen a loon, then checked again. It was a cormorant: a long-necked, black-feathered, fish-eating diving bird. A double-crested cormorant.

"I mean," I said, misreading the book, "I saw a double-breasted cormorant." My birding was full of errors, but I loved it. I met people who went birding. That first year when I went out with them, I identified a number of double-breasted cormorants.

No one corrected me.

"There goes another double-breasted!" I'd call. The other birders must have been annoyed, or just embarrassed. Maybe—I console myself with this—in a field where one can spot a bristle-thighed curlew, a white-eared hummingbird, or a flame-headed oriole, anything seemed possible, and it might have crossed their minds that just possibly I knew something they hadn't heard of yet. Breasts on a bird. A bird in a suit.

The last double-breasted I identified flew close to the water as I sang out its name and a friend swung his binoculars in the bird's direction, nearly knocking me flat.

"Why did you do that?" I asked him.

"To catch a look at the breasts," he said. Then he told me the true name. He opened his bird book and pointed to the feathers curling off the back of the breeding bird's head. The double crests.

My mother-in-law gave me a brand-new pair of binoculars that highly magnified everything, and I couldn't quite tell the size of the birds anymore. I would find a bird, the binoculars would magnify it, and it seemed crow-sized to me. A crow-sized sparrow. Out on salt water, I discovered loons the size of robins.

The old bird guide presented problems. Until you have a grasp of bird families, where do you start? I would see a warbler, wouldn't have any idea it was a warbler, and look under "oriole," searching for an especially petite oriole. But in a cabin without electricity my children and my husband and I spent winter hours reading around kerosene lamps. I began to study the book. I read it cover to cover, then I read it again. I looked at the pictures and learned that birds go together in families, that the families have common features, and they are found in habitats. You can look at a piece of land at a particular time of year and have a good idea what birds might be there.

After a few years, in another flourish of confidence,

I joined the local Christmas bird count. I was given my own area to survey, a road with fields on either side, framed at their edges by alders and young maples. It was January, windy, knife-cold. I arrived at dawn wearing two wool hats and carrying a dozen homemade donuts that I had bought at a diner up on Route 1. They were still warm and smelled of nutmeg. By noon I had eaten the donuts and had identified the only bird that had flown my way: a blue jay. By three o'clock, as the sun gave up and went down, one more jay flew across one more snow-crusted, wind-scraped field.

The next year I was given West Bay in Gouldsboro. Out of the wind off the open water, it was a shelter for winter ducks. Counting common goldeneyes, I was trying with the force of my will to make them keep their wings down, not to dive, and not to swim in front of the buffleheads, which I was also counting along with the few scoters that had joined them and were dipping underwater and coming up somewhere else. There were more than two hundred ducks in the bay. I decided to map the bay in my mind—each four square yards would contain approximately so many ducks—and I set about doing just that, and came up with a number for each species.

"Nice raft of ducks," said a voice beside me. I turned to see the leader of the bird count standing next to me, his binoculars scanning the tumultuous scene. I hadn't heard his approach, but I wished, then, he had offered me the sere fields again with no more than two blue jays and plenty of time to eat donuts. I told him the numbers of goldeneyes; buffleheads; and black, surf, and white-winged scoters I had counted.

"Sounds about right," he said. "Anything else?"

About right? I was thrilled. "I've checked around," I said with new confidence. "I don't see anything."

"What about," he said, slowly scanning the trees on the other side of the bay, "that bald eagle? Up there in the pine? Its head looks like a clump of snow on a branch. But it's moving. See it?"

Today I know more about birds than I did. I know about their outline and their manner of flight. I don't always get it right. I never will. But when I catch the silhouette of a bird in the air or on the water, something about it often triggers the name, as if the sight of the bird matched a template I carry in my brain, in the place that stores patterns. This knowledge is like grace, a reward I did not earn. But that's the way grace comes.

We lived in a fishing community. Our neighbors knew lots of things—practical, smart, lifesaving things. In those early days, when so much was new to me, I learned to trust what I saw by finding references to them in books, deferring to the written word. As I got to know my neighbors, I noticed that they were more attuned to their experience, and to the experiences of their parents and grandparents and the people they worked with. They passed things along verbally. This was the '70s, and in that small harbor town we still had a culture based on generations making a living from the sea. My neighbors' experiences were rich in detail and, if they had been written down, would have been too heavy to lift. But they were carried in their heads, lightly.

I used to stop in to visit with Elaine and George Lowell. I cut fish in the canning factory with Elaine, who, if I arrived at their house in the early afternoon, at dinner-time, would invite me to share whatever it was they were eating. Sometimes she took home a mackerel that had come in on the conveyor belt with the herring, and she'd bake it in milk and serve it with potatoes.

George had been a fisherman all his life until his heart began to give out. He put on weight and could barely move from chair to chair in the house, let alone walk down to the harbor and row the dingy to his boat. He was a smart, cagey, storytelling man who loved an audi-ence. And I loved his stories about fishing beyond the harbor light, out where the water is deep and change-able. George's father had been a fisherman. So had his grandfather. As a boy, he learned most of what there was to know about boats. He also learned to read the signs the water offers, and the air above it: the clues that can mean schooling fish or a coming storm, or, I suppose, hundreds of other things. George also knew, as all the good fishermen down at the harbor did, something of what the ground looked like under the water. He carried in his head a relief map of edges and troughs. A template of sorts.

He rigged his boat for lobstering and for long-lining, depending on the season. He had been a good fisherman in a time when there were fewer nautical instruments than there are today, which meant he was on his own more. And he was, of course, proud of what he knew.

As we sat in his living room one afternoon, he leaned back in his recliner and told me about a time he went fishing for cod.

"That's when I saw a humpback whale die," he said. "It was making a moaning noise, like a human in terrible agony."

A school of swordfish had surrounded the whale like a pack of wolves, he told me, and the bloodied animal headed for the shallow water of the banks, and those fish just followed it in. "I'll never forget that sound," he said. "It must have been in some god-awful pain."

I was stunned. I had not read about swordfish attacking whales, and I thought he must have gotten it wrong.

Maybe sharks. Maybe a pod of killer whales. Swordfish don't eat whales, so why bother to attack one? It didn't make sense.

"But swordfish have no reason to kill whales," I protested.

"None that we know of, dear," he said, shifting himself in his recliner. "But we're not swordfish."

Years later, leafing through a copy of a wildlife magazine, I came upon a paragraph about the few reports of swordfish attacking whales. When I phoned a marine biologist to get his opinion, he started by saying, "I have enormous respect for fishermen." Then he said that there were occasional reports that he knew about of swordfish attacking ships, breaking their swords off in wooden hulls. No one knew why it happened. And whales, well, he had heard of it. He didn't know what to think. But the noise the dying whale made? Where would that have come from?

I do not know what George saw or heard. But I know he knew the fishing grounds where he worked. He was a witness at a time out on the water when understanding what you saw could save your life.

Learning about something, staying with what engages our attention, staying beyond the naming of it, is like the layering of sediment. Over time, what we know acquires weight and permanence and we become, instead of watchers, witnesses, heavy with the gravity of what is revealed to us and what we have chosen to carry of it.

Three weeks ago I released a fledged cedar waxwing. For more than a decade, I was a licensed wild bird rehabilitator. I don't take birds now. But sometimes a person hears of the work I used to do and shows up with a bird, and I accept it.

The waxwing was a nestling brought by a woman who had befriended an eighty-five-year-old man who lived alone and spent his time looking at birds outside his big kitchen window. He had phoned to tell her that a pair of cedar waxwings had picked their four young up out of a nest on the other side of the road and set them in a stand of brush and trees on his property. They were getting away from house cats, he said.

Then he saw one of the parents go down under the

wheel of a car, and soon after the other disappeared. He sat at the window and watched the young waxwings huddling together on a branch for two days. The night he called, the woman went right over, took a flashlight, and climbed into the brush. Two of the young birds had died, one was dying, and one would survive.

The story is impossible.

It did not happen.

Songbird young can't be safely coaxed to leave their nests until they are ready to go, and their parents have never been reported to carry them. Impossible. But what did the old man see? What did he miss? Had he fallen asleep, concerned for the birds across the road, and dreamed this?

And how did the nestlings—who were unable to fly and could barely hop—end up clinging together on a branch?

When you take care of a young bird, before you release it, you want to know the whole story, the odd unraveling of its particular narrative. You want to hear especially the part you didn't share with it, the part that is the dark side of the miracle that brought the bird to you, and the subsequent miracle that you didn't kill it by mistake, that it somehow thrived in your vigilant presence.

I cared for the waxwing for three weeks and released it, healthy and ready to go, into the nearby trees where other waxwings immediately received it. Before I could decide which bird it was, they flew.

A woman from the next town called yesterday to say she had found a baby bird in a field, mourning its parent.

"It's doing what?"

"Mourning. It's mourning its parent. The parent is dead."

"How is it doing this?" I asked.

"It's standing on the mother's body."

"Oh."

"It's hunched over its mother who is dead in the field, and there are feathers all over the place. It just keeps flying back to her . . . it doesn't want to leave."

"It's a hawk," I told her. "It's eating another bird."

"I don't think so," she said, "because I got to within ten feet and it wouldn't fly. It just clung to her. Also they have the same feathers."

"Yes?"

"They're brown. "

Inwardly, I groaned. But something was off. The hawk shouldn't let her get that close.

"Why don't I meet you at the field?" I said. "You can show me where the bird is."

When I stepped out of the car, she was standing at the side of the road with a toddler in her arms, a blond little boy, and the bird—a young Cooper's hawk—was feeding on the body of an immature herring gull. As we stood and watched, other people gathered around.

Soon we were a small crowd talking about hawks. The Cooper's lifted off the gull, flew to a fence, settled, then flew back to the gull. Its flight seemed to me direct and strong. A Cooper's is a woodland hawk that hunts by weaving its way through the trees, ruddering its long tail, and dropping down on songbirds. Speed and surprise are its talents. A healthy Cooper's does not feed in an open field with a human audience. The gull had most likely not been killed by this hawk but had died of other causes. It lay on its breast. The hawk had pierced the left shoulder and was picking its way to the heart and lungs.

I walked over to the bird, looked at it, and walked back to report.

"It seems okay," I said. "It's hungry. Young hawks sometimes have trouble finding enough food."

"I think its wing is injured," the woman with the child said. "When I walked over this morning one of its wings hung down."

"I think it's mantling," I told her, and explained how hawks try to protect food from being stolen from them by shawling their wings around it. I was watching her hold her son, remembering holding my own son at that tender age, and how alert I was to every living thing that I thought might be in danger, that might need my help. I couldn't bear the thought that my son was living in a world in which harm could come without reason or warning.

A man joined our group and began a story about a great blue heron on a dock at night in the Florida Keys.

"So I came up on deck and there in the moonlight was this great big great blue heron. It was diving off the dock into the water catching fish. When I heard the first splash, I thought a drunk had fallen in . . ."

"Something's wrong with the hawk," the woman insisted.

"Herons don't dive," I said.

"That's what I thought, too, but then it did it again . . ."

"Herons never dive—" I said.

"The hawk's sick. I'm sure of it," she interrupted.

"Okay. I'll go take another look," I said. I could feel the eyes of these good people on my back, and the weight of their conviction—with the exception of the woman holding the child and perhaps the man who saw the diving heron—that I was going to figure this out and do something sensible about it. That it was a problem with a solution.

A first-year Cooper's is a hot-wired bird, long and thin and fast, with a wedge-shaped head and brass-colored eyes. It looks like what it's made for: killing other birds, master of the quick sprint and hairpin turn. The young bird, locked on the gull, lifted its head. It stared at me with one fine eye and one eye filled with blackness. The damaged eye was flicking. I knew then that the bird couldn't see my outline against the sky. I must have appeared all fractures and kaleidoscopic light. A hawk with eyes that can't synchronize can't make a kill.

The bird's talons were deep in the feathers of the gull, holding open the red tear it had made. It stared up at me and I stared back, and the eye filled with the slack pupil kept jolting.

"I'm sorry," I whispered. "I am so sorry." I turned and walked back to the crowd.

"You're right," I said to the woman.

"I knew it," she said.

I told the group what I had seen. "Maybe it was injured. Maybe it was born like that," I said.

"What do we do now?" someone asked.

"Unfortunately, nothing," I said. "There is nothing we can do. The bird's too fast to catch and too damaged to survive."

Silently, we all turned and stared at the hawk ripping ferociously at the gull. Small gusts of feathers floated from its work.

Then we went home.

What were the chances that the Cooper's hawk would come back to the field? That it would be slow to rise off the body of the gull? That I would go there one more time, summoned by the woman with the child? I pictured myself walking over that field again. This time I lean down and snatch the bird, take it by the legs just above the talons, gather one flailing wing and fold it against my body, and tuck the other wing against my elbow, gathering, folding it into my arms.

That night I woke up and stepped outside and stood in the wet grass. The stars were out. The night was still. It was the time of year when thrushes, migrating in flocks, call back and forth to one another. The quick, high, haunting sounds they make keep them in touch. Sometimes we can hear them when they pass low overhead and it seems as if, for a second or two, we share with them their urgency and risk, their desire not to lose each other in the dark. I listened, but everything was quiet, and I began to think about the Cooper's hawk again, perched somewhere on a limb in the woods, asleep, its damaged face tucked into the feathers of its shoulder.

Years ago I stood under the stars, unsure of my own relationship to gravity. Now I know a jumbled handful of things about this place where I have lived most of my life. The weight of it keeps me here.

Tree

The house I live in sits at the edge of a small field, which is surrounded by trees. They are mostly softwoods, white pines and red spruces, northern white cedars, balsam firs, hemlocks, and two or three tamaracks. The white pines, which I am told were saplings the year Lincoln delivered his second inaugural, are especially tall. They cast shadows across the field, reaching up straight and close together like a quiver of gigantic arrows, like a memory of trees before they bore the king's mark, before they were felled to hold aloft the sails of an empire.

On the other side of the town road, the land has been clear-cut. Down at the marsh behind my house, the land's been overcut, the brush and broken trees that are left an impenetrable thicket of waste. Nothing has been cut on my land for a long, long time, except to make this little clearing.

A friend once asked me if the big trees and the tiny field made me feel hemmed in. I don't think so, I told him. I wasn't sure why. Now I believe it is because an old dead pine about sixty feet tall points above a copse of cedars and firs. It stands south of the kitchen windows. I see it every time I look outside. Over the years, it has trained my vision upward, into the open sky and the weather.

Its long snags once stretched to the west. Most of them have fallen, and it looks less like a fish's backbone and more like a thrust of index finger—fierce and stark. While the other trees swing their branches in the wind, the old pine offers only a brittle tremor. When snow clings in drifts to the other trees, the old tree accepts a mere cup of it, stuck between the silvered trunk and a stub.

One could say it refuses adornment and disapproves of dancing, that it is an alarming old Calvinist—a most terribly alive dead tree. And one could say it's a fine bird perch. It has, in fact, been a generous teacher. As I write this, a flicker has latched itself to the tree's skinny trunk. I watch the bird dart its head around to one side and shout "wicka-wicka-wicka," then fly off. An hour ago, two resident pileated woodpeckers shimmied up the tree. They were yelling "kuk-kuk-kuk-kuk," a brash call, much like the flicker's. But if you hear the calls one after the other, an undertone of complaint reveals itself in the flicker's, while the pileated's sound is big and confident.

Last February, a male white-winged crossbill stood at the top of the tree and sang a sharp twitter. The temperature was dropping every night, and here was this bird in the morning claiming territory, as if he thought he had a nest somewhere. I read about crossbills and learned that he did indeed have a nest. Probably on a spruce, probably about ten feet up, and out on a branch. But I never found it. And I never saw his mate. He sang from the old tree every day for four cold weeks.

A band of crows flew down late last winter after the crossbill left. They gorged themselves on the cracked corn I threw out in the field for the turkeys. Their sentinel took its solitary place on one of the lower snags of the tree. A silent bird, it kept an eye out as the others jabbed in the melting snow. Spring came on, and the sentinel watched the others shout and frolic; sometimes they scooted on their sides in the slush, jumped up and walked around each other with bow-legged swaggers, or they slapped wet snow on themselves with their wings as if it were water.

One day the flock and the sentinel and the snow disappeared. The ground was muddy, the little pond in the field was overflowing, and whispered crow talk issued from somewhere in the woods behind the old tree. It sounded like a conversation between two. In a week, the pair showed itself. The birds perched in a red maple as it flowered. They sat wing to wing, nuzzling each other's heads and backs with their beaks.

Robins flew in but didn't stay. White-throated sparrows sang, but the songs stopped. The mourning doves left. Crows pillage other birds' nests, and one day I found a naked half-eaten squab on the driveway.

As spring turned to early summer, a single crow perched on a stub of the old tree, its wings held up around its head like hunched shoulders. The body language looked to me as if the bird felt ill-tempered, worn out. A few weeks of fledgling crow-scream bothered the place, but at last, the woods fell silent, the crows disappeared, and the robins came back. A big red-breasted male sang from the top of the old tree. A white-throated sparrow family found a spot to nest somewhere on the ground in the cedar brush near its base, and the male intoned its lovely plainsong. A blue-headed vireo sang its relentless monologue from tree to tree all around the green field.

One summer I bought thirty goldfish at the pet store in town, slipped them into the pond at the bottom of the field, and invited everyone who stopped in to come down and sit with me to watch the jewel-like fish swimming among the lily pads. I couldn't get over how beautiful they were. They grew quickly and they survived a winter under the ice.

The next summer, a kingfisher flew in to the old tree. It was a female, with a belt of rust-colored feathers across her chest. She was studying the pond. When I heard her rattling call, I dropped what I was doing and sprinted to save my fish, shouting to scare the bird off. But she came back. It became a ritual: She would land on the tree, rattle, and I would come running. Sometimes friends were here. They looked around, startled, maybe a little embarrassed. They had no idea what was happening. My kids got used to it.

"There she goes again," they'd say, as if I were the noon whistle.

Most often, I arrived late, just in time to see the kingfisher splash between the lilies. She shot out of the water with a bright orange flash in her beak, flew back to her perch on the old tree, and whacked the gorgeous, desperate fish around to stun it. Then, when it went limp, she ate it. One by one, she swallowed all my fish.

Mourning doves, the males with a wash of pink on their breasts, often perch on the tree, gray on gray, while the sky beyond them turns rosy on late summer evenings. Slowly, as the light leaves, the doves begin to look more and more like the branch stubs. Just at the moment when I can no longer distinguish them from the tree itself, they take off to safer roosts.

A forester who is a friend came by last week to talk about cutting some fir to let light in for the young white pines. He looked across the field and said, "Nice tree," and I looked around to find the one he was talking about.

"Which one?" I asked him.

"The dead pine," he said.

"Since when do foresters like dead trees?"

"We had a dead elm in our yard when our kids were small," he said. "We got all sorts of birds coming to it."

"Like what?" I asked.

"It had a hole where a limb had fallen off, and one summer pileated woodpeckers nested in it. It drew birds all year long—swallows, robins, evening grosbeaks. When it collapsed, we were pretty disappointed."

"That old pine will be here," I told him, "probably forever."

He smiled. "You can't go out and buy one like it . . . perches, beetle larvae, ants . . . good stuff."

After he left, I worried. Sure, my tree grew thinner and more insistently pointed every year, but it hadn't occurred to me that it might fall. I pushed my way through the clumps of wet fir and cedar to the old tree's base to get a closer look. I needed to be sure that it was okay. There, in the gloom of the thick woods, I saw my tree up close for the first time, and a life I hadn't known about— a past I hadn't been curious enough to ask about— presented itself no more than a few inches from my face. Down the trunk ran a lightning scar. It was deep and wide. The tree had been burned to the heartwood, which was pitted and grooved and dark. To mend itself, it had grown a thick, smooth, milky-white ridge of living tissue on either side of the scar. But with that strike, its trunk had lost a third of its bark.

When had this happened? Maybe fifty years ago. Maybe more. I looked around at the litter on the ground, the stuff the tree has been dropping for years: branches the size of ribs and tusks, wrinkled sheets of bark as tough as elephant knees. At the base was a large hole. I stuck my hand in, reached up, and found no end to it.

Leaning against the damaged trunk, I closed my eyes and breathed in the smell of rotten wood. Then I looked up to the pointing finger and saw that it was not the original trunk. The original was a few feet above my head, stunted, withered. When my tree was a mere adolescent, years before the lightning strike, a pine weevil, a beetle with spotted, dull brown wing coverts, had laid its eggs in the terminal shoot, just below the terminal bud, the place where a tree grows. No tree grows from the base. Carve your initials into a sapling and they will be at the same height as long as the tree stands. The part that reaches farther into the sky every year is the bud, and it is that which a weevil smaller than a shelled peanut killed on my tree.

But, slowly—because it had no intention of dying—the tree reached one of its main branches upward to take the place of the dead trunk, fighting gravity's heavy tug as it transformed its horizontal into vertical. It converted that branch to a new trunk and kept on growing.

The branch grew thick. Many side branches sprang from it, and for years this crippled tree thrived. Until lightning scalded it. And long-horned beetles bored holes into the dead wood. They laid eggs. The larvae hatched, crawled around in the heartwood, pupated, then emerged flying to lay more eggs in the tree. Carpenter ants found the bark loosened by the longhorns. They made tunnels under it and what fell from beneath the bark was frass—powdery insect dung—and kerf—a fine, dry sawdust.

Now great piles of frass and kerf lie in wet mounds around the base. Pileated woodpecker holes pit the trunk as the birds pry the tree apart searching for larvae and ants. Finally, I can't help but see that my tree is braced between a cedar and a fir. Like nurses in end-of-life care, they hold it aloft.

I find myself getting up in the dark now to stand by the south windows down in the kitchen, to look into the sky to find the tree, to make sure it's still there. I've never seen a bird on it at night, but it may be at its most dramatic then, spectral, with the clouds skimming behind it. Sometimes, as I stand there, the moon emerges to glaze the old tree in a shock of clean, cold light, and I think, this tree is going to last forever.

Big Fish

A culvert runs under the bridge at the Cross Road. It is six feet in diameter. At low tide it carries heath water from upland streams into the head of Morgan Bay. At high tide it sends salt water a quarter of a mile into the marsh and the streams beyond. It lies in a bed of granite riprap, beside a gentle outcrop on the bay side, and on a hot day in summer this ancient Ellsworth schist is warm from the sun. At high tide, you can lie back against its received heat and let your heels rest in the sloshing water. The water thrums through the culvert.

When a car goes over the bridge above, the pipe vibrates, a deep, hollow sound.

At the bay side, a pool directly beneath the culvert holds water even at dead low. If you stand on the road and look down through that gritty water you see a jumble of barnacle-encrusted rocks over which green crabs and minnows mull about, caught in the bowl by the receding tide.

At high tide, this is the place to swim after work. Neighbors come down in various attire to plop themselves in the water in front of the culvert. Some swim through it to the marsh. Except during spring tides, there is always headroom in the pipe. The salt water has come in across acres of dark bay mud. It carries the warmth the mud absorbed from the sun at low tide.

Young herring swim by. They travel together in long ribbon-like schools following close to the mud banks and rocks. They weave through the Spartina grasses at high tide. Every so often they fling themselves into the air and slap down like sudden tiny rainsqualls as schools of menhaden and mackerel strike them from below.

In early summer, this water is a soup swarming with

the larvae of jellyfish and barnacles and krill. You can dip your hands into it and cup them and come up with handfuls of new life. The herring will take these larvae, and the larger fish will take the herring, and the birds will take the larger fish. Everyone out here, except for the human swimmers, is eating everyone else.

Two kingfishers clatter across the water and perch together on the rock that stands in the bay a short swim from the culvert. They stare into the water, waiting for a fish to swim into the rock's shadow.

Ospreys coast back and forth over the open water. One draws its wings in, tilts, and drops. It rakes its talons into the water with a quick punch. Then the bird lifts, hovering as it adjusts the thrashing slick body of a fish, and carries it horizontally, headfirst, held tight and straight in its pebble-rough feet. It shakes the water out of its feathers as it flies.

In high summer, striped bass cruise close to shore. The mackerel schools are following the smaller fish. The stripers are hunting the mackerel. Every now and then, the water explodes, and goes quiet.

My neighbors and I hang in the water, gabbing. No

one swims for long. Ten minutes, twenty minutes, then we go home.

After we leave, the rush of living and dying continues. Even at night, blue herons flap down, furl their wings up, and step to the water's edge to catch fish whose silver sides glint with reflected moonlight. And in the long summer gloaming black ducks pad over the mud gorging on snails.

Beyond Morgan Bay, out on the eastern side of Hardwood Island, a grid of steel salmon cages bobs in the water. Tides and currents slosh through it. Netting covers the cages, and underneath them the growing salmon turn circles in net bowls, with more layers of netting hung below them to keep out harbor seals. The penned fish are not true relatives of the wild Atlantic salmon that used to swim up Maine rivers to spawn. Bred of a number of populations brought in from rivers on both sides of the Atlantic, they are man-made fish, in the sense that the eggs and milt of these subspecies would not have met and mixed naturally in a wild river. Instead, the eggs are fertilized in a laboratory, then incubated in trays. The fry live in rearing tanks. When they have grown large enough, they are transported out to the pens such as those by Hardwood Island. There they fatten and are harvested.

This procedure of combining different salmon strains may seem a small matter, but here in Maine, it can undermine the years of hard work to restore the original fish to home rivers. The first threat comes from the possibility that a genetically mixed pen-raised rogue might swim upriver with the few survivors of the wild stock, and breed. The second is that the diseases and parasites carried in penned-reared fish will infect the wild stock. Industrially raised, sprayed with fungicides, doused with antibiotics, penned salmon—lovely fish to look at—are lives in crisis: packed tightly, kept alive with drugs.

Perhaps they don't have the skills to survive in the open sea. Perhaps. But a wild Atlantic salmon headed to its home river, the Penobscot, say, or the Dennys or the Narraguagus, is a sleek, ocean-smart fish, and extremely rare.

Sometimes the big pens out beyond the islands are ripped apart by seals or a storm, and the fish funnel through the sprung nets and disappear into the bay. We lose track of them. We have no idea what they will do or where they will go. Which—if any—buried instinct will come into play? There is something touching—even tragic—about incarcerated fish suddenly freed into a life that was once a birthright.

One lazy afternoon in August, I walked my springer, William, down to the bay. It was low tide. We stopped at the bridge and my gaze drifted into the pool by the culvert. I noticed what seemed to be a large shadow hovering within it. I looked into the sky. It was cloudless. I looked into the pool again, really looked this time. What took shape were four huge fish with blunt caudal fins turning slow circles in the small water. They were salmon. They were about three feet long and shaped like torpedoes.

William and I ran back to the house and I called a fish biologist I know. He told me to take a good look at the dorsal fins. The dorsal fin on a penned salmon is tattered with fungus, he said. "But remember," he added, "no one is allowed to catch free-swimming salmon in Maine these days whether they are pen-raised or wild. It's against the law for now. We have to protect all free-swimming salmon because we are gambling that the wild fish will come back. We can't risk the loss of a single one."

"Okay," I said. I hung up and ran back to the bay. The fish were the color of the rocks at the bottom of the pool, a mottled gray. They were swimming lazily, half-asleep in the oxygen-starved water, and, yes, their dorsal fins were covered in a filmy white bloom. I stood watching them, astonished that their instinct had brought them here, for they must have followed the scent of fresh water that came into the bay from the upland streams, a tiny thread traced with sweetness in all that salt. But these shallow streams were no place for fish like this. I dashed up the road again, stopped in to tell my neighbor, Susan, about the extraordinary fish, ran home to grab my binoculars, then walked back down.

Voices reached me before I got there. A man I had never seen before in a wet T-shirt and shorts, sneakers and a baseball cap, was standing astride the pool with a big grin on his face. He must have been in his seventies, with two little boys, perhaps his grandchildren, running and yelping in glee. He had brought down a big red and white cooler and a fish identification book. I watched him step into the pool, lean over, and make wide grabbing gestures. The fish were pressing themselves against the sharp rocks at the bottom to escape. They had nowhere else to go.

He leaned in deeper, lithe and quick, as if he were suddenly a young hunter, and he rummaged deep. He got a thrash of water in his face. But he stepped to the center of the pool, leaned down again, snatched, and stood up with a salmon pressed against his chest. It beat against his T-shirt. The kids screamed, and blood from the fish hit him in the face as he carried it out of the pool and tried to shove it into the cooler. It was too big. It flipped and fell on the rocks, cut its belly, and plopped back into the pool. In a flash, he was after it, lunging into the pool in his soaked sneakers. Again, he rummaged around, grabbing here and there in the churned-up water. He found the fish and lifted it high.

Susan had come up behind me.

"Oh, my god," she said quietly.

"I think that's against the law!" I shouted above the children's screams.

"Why?" he shouted back.

"Because it's a salmon. You're not allowed to catch salmon anymore."

"How do you know it's a salmon?" he yelled, still holding the fish. But once more, it slipped away from him.

Before I could explain to him what a salmon looked like, how it looked exactly like the fish he was holding against his chest, Susan and I turned to the sound of bare feet slapping down the road. A neighbor who lived in a house on the hill came running toward us wearing cut-off jeans and carrying a knife. He was young and strong and he leaped over the guardrail, rushed across the riprap, and jumped with both feet into the pool, onto the crusted barnacles and the rocks. Plunging in past his shoulders, he let his face go under, and lifted up a fish, held it against his chest and slit its throat.

The tide came in that night. The little pool by the culvert lay deep under water. Out of our midst had appeared two hunters. We saw them move with an irruptive, opportunistic joy. They were not wild men, and these were not wild fish—but something in the fish and in the men had not been entirely tamed away. The fish had come in, nosing after sweet water as if they were trying to remember why, and this behavior stirred in the men a heart-drumming moment of frenzy.

That night, the scent of grilled salmon drifted over the Cross Road and lifted into the still air, proclaiming a gift from the sea.

Ice

This morning ice stretches across the bay at dead low like a glaze of varnish and makes the dark November mud shine. When the tide comes in, it shatters the ice and sweeps it against the rocks at the shore.

I walk past the tall bare hardwoods, past the pin cherries and viburnums with their leaves gone, to stand at the rocks. Thousands of ice slivers undulate in the shifting water at my feet, making delicate pins-and-needles sounds as they jumble against each other. The sounds are somewhat—but not quite—reminiscent of the calls back and forth of small birds in flocks heading south in the dark, flying not far above the trees. The voices are so high and thin, you might think you imagined them. But those birds—the black-throated green, chestnut-sided, and bay-breasted warblers; the Swainson's thrushes, the red-eyed and blue-headed vireos—are gone.

The ice has just arrived.

In a long winter, ice sometimes stretches all the way to Jed Island, two and a half miles down the bay. We who live here walk in narrow daylight hours to stand at the bridge at the culvert, to let the wind, shearing down the length of the snow-covered bay, blast our faces and tear through our coats and scarves. The world around us is stark and fierce, as if we had come into the heart of the Arctic.

At night when storms shriek at the corners of our houses, the ice at the bay in the first light is a train wreck, a pile-up of white boxcars, a sprawl of icicle-dripping flatbeds. But on the next windless day, the tide comes in beneath the broken pieces, and the beautiful pale green water rises gently between them. It pools on their surfaces, smoothes their edges, binds the ice fast to itself again. Dozens of times a winter the ice fractures apart, heals, and grows thicker.

These are the nights we let ourselves think that winter—this particular winter—will be the one that goes on forever. We start to lose the memory of what spring smells like, the feel of summer's warmth against our skin.

In March, the ice shifts over and over in its shallow bed. It sounds as if it is groaning, as if it can't get comfortable. Day after day, it melts. It freezes. Melts. Then a rough spring tide knocks the whole thing to pieces. One day, open water appears, blue-black and puckered with sharp waves.

A few weeks later, I hike along the bay, seeing for the first time in months the seaweed hanging from the rocks, bright mustard-yellow fringes of knotted wrack. The water sloshes and slaps at the shore. Up ahead, on a bed of Spartina grass roots, I hear the piercing two-note cry of a killdeer, a bird just returned from the south.

It knows what I keep having to relearn: that time— moving forward—does circle. It is in the circling where

I lose confidence. That spring will come round. As will summer. Then fall. Then, once again, birds go and ice comes. To the killdeer the circle is what time is all about. I suspect it knows nothing of time moving forward, that we step into the future and away from the past, the part that I know best.

Trapped

In the small field before my garden, Ray touches a match to a brush pile. He gives it a little chaser of kerosene and the fire starts gulping down wet wood with a roar. I've hired him to cut some trees with his chain saw, limb and chunk them, then drag them to the fire. I'm cutting small trees with a hand saw and lugging them to the burn pile along with some brush that has been lying around for years. It is late March, a day lacquered in last night's cold rain.

Ray is my neighbor. He lives with his family up on the East Blue Hill Road, and he owns the best view in

Surry: Morgan Bay below, then the thin peninsula of Newbury Neck, Union River Bay, the shoreline of Trenton, and up against the sky like blue cardboard cutouts, the stern mountains of Acadia. People driving the road below the house turn to look at the water and the mountains and nearly lose their grip on the steering wheel. It is that startling. Then it is gone.

Ray has been cutting trees, tilling gardens, plowing driveways, and haying for over twenty years, ever since he decided he did not like teaching school.

Today we work in separate parts of my woodlot and the fire gobbles up everything we throw in. The smell of burning trees infuses the air and soaks into our clothes along with the sharp scent of fresh-cut cedar and spruce. The rain begins again and we work in it. It is a good feeling to cut and pull and throw. Good to be at work with Ray working nearby, and the fire going strong.

When I first knew him, Ray trapped coyotes. He set his traps above the high-tide line on his property down at the bay. He hitched the trap chains around pieces of driftwood, wedged the jaws open between a few stones, and baited them. The coyotes, following the flotsam the bay gives up, trotting along the edge of the water at night, couldn't miss them.

In those same years, I walked my terrier, Sadie, at the bay. She liked the tide line because it collected things, and I liked to walk her there because I could look for birds out on the water as she inspected the tumbled coils of sea wrack. One afternoon, we turned right instead of left, to walk at the edge of the water below Ray's land. When Sadie cried out, I dashed for her. A trap was clamped on to her left front paw. A trapped coyote waits as still as a stone, but my dog was pulling and thrashing and the sounds out of her throat were piercing, ragged. I grabbed her. She bit me. I held on, braced myself against a rock and tired to pry open the jaws of the trap. Frothing, she bit me again. I was screaming at her to stop screaming and biting. We rolled together over the rotted seaweed, and I can't imagine what we must have looked and sounded like from any distance.

I managed to raise the upper jaw a half an inch. She yanked herself free.

"Sadie," I said and held out my hand. But she would have none of it. She backed away. She refused to look at me, but turned instead, and limping along the shore, headed for home by herself. I watched her low-slung frizzy shape hobble to the road. Enraged, I ripped the trap and chain from the log and searched for a name. No one can legally set a trap without putting his initials on it somewhere. I didn't find anything, so I slung it over my shoulder, walked home, and hung it on a nail in the cellar. I didn't know for sure who had set the trap, and, at the time, I didn't much care.

"What happened to Sadie?" my son asked.

"She got caught in a leghold trap," I told him. She let me examine her foot. The trap did not break the skin or the fine bones of her lovely toes.

A month later, on a Saturday morning, there was a brisk knock at the front door. It was Ray.

"I'm missing a trap," he said. He had been cutting in the woods and smelled of fresh pinesap.

Now, to be honest, Ray and I had a little bit of history between us. In those days, I was one of the founding members of the Surry Wetlands Association. We were a group trying to save undeveloped land at the bay, and he told me that he didn't much like the idea of saving wild places. He thought it was a sentimental way to look at land, an idea inspired mostly by people who were not born here, people who had never worked the land, people who had not done anything to stop the ruin in their own home places. Surry was still a workingman's town for him, with resources for the taking in all the traditional ways. He had watched "No Trespassing" signs go up where he used to hunt, and despite the jobs he took from these new people, he thought the exclusion, the shutting down of land, was arrogant.

"I've got a trap down cellar but it doesn't have a name on it," I told him.

"If it's mine, it does," he said.

I marched down to the cellar and returned with it and thrust it into his hand. At the link where the chain met the jaws, he pulled out a thin coil of tin I had not seen. It was stamped "R.M."

"That's me," he said, pointing to the initials. "R.M. That's me. I spent half a day looking for that coyote. I could take you to court. It's not legal pulling other people's traps. And I get a hundred dollars a pelt. You lost me a hundred dollars and a half-day's work."

I knew enough to forgo an argument on a trapped animal's fear and pain. Or an argument about how unjust it is for people to wear the skins and furs of wild animals as statements of fashion. Ray was taking the wild lives that, in a sense, belonged to all of us or to none of us, and selling them away to people he wouldn't particularly like or respect.

"Ray," I said. "Take a look at where we live. Land gets sold. Houses get built. You're trapping a few feet from the high-tide line and you've got neighbors and they walk the bay. They take their kids and their dogs out there. Walter, up on the hill, has a half-dozen barn cats with three legs thanks to your traps. We've changed, Ray. Trapping is a lousy idea here."

"You seem to know quite a bit about what I should be doing," he said.

"My dog was caught in this trap. It'll happen again with someone else's dog. I'm being realistic."

"Realistic. So that's what you call your save-the-marsh business? Your trap-stealing business?" My daughter came out of her bedroom and stood at the top of the stairs looking down.

"You people give us a good laugh. You 'wetlands' people. We laugh at that a little bit, you know."

"We're funny?" I asked.

"Yup, you're kind of funny," he said. Then he held out his hands, which were thick and rough, a workingman's hands. "What do you see?" he demanded.

"Hands," I said.

"Calluses," he corrected. "What you see are calluses, and I got them from honest work. I don't have time to sit up in my house thinking about saving marshes."

"Ray," I said, and I held out my hands. "I write. I type all day. That's how I make money. I mean, not very much money, but look at the tip of my finger. There, right there. That is a callus."

He looked at my hands. He relaxed and laughed.

"Well, I can't see it," he said. "If you say so, I'll believe you, but it's pretty small."

Ray and I both know the wild land that is left here, maybe better than most, because we have spent a lot of time on it. But we know it differently. We see it differently.

That evening, I remembered a town meeting some years before. Neighbors and I had founded the Surry Wetlands Association, to which Ray had alluded. We were the "wetlands people," and probably will always be as long as we live in this town. I am honored by the moniker, but in truth, our plans were modest, although we chose the word *association* because we thought it implied many, and we were few—ten people, full count.

In those first years, we slogged into many watery places and met in each other's living rooms to talk about how a group such as ours might work to save some of them. Surry looks southeast into two bays, but even without its salt water, it is soggy with soaks, spring pools, ponds, lakes, streams and brooks, wet meadows, a heath, a lagg, and swamps. We explored many of them, tangled habitats dense with signs of wildlife.

We decided to write a letter to the town, explaining that our association was interested in protecting wetlands. The letter went out at the same time the selectmen called a special meeting to cover two pressing topics. The first was a number of barking dog complaints. The second was that the state required a town conservation plan with designated wildlife habitat areas.

Everyone in our group arrived for the meeting at the school gymnasium and sat down in a row on metal fold-out chairs. The people who owned the barking dogs filed in, fifteen men, staying close together. I had never seen them before. They took seats at the back of the room. You could tell by the body language—a bit of swagger—that they had chewed the dog issue over among themselves. Looking back, I think that most of them who came to defend themselves and their pets—this barking dog constituency—were probably shy at heart, people not given to public address. They arrived prepared for a tussle.

The longest serving selectman opened the meeting. He introduced the agenda: barking dogs, first; comprehensive plan, second. He also paused to acknowledge the presence of our group, the Surry Wetlands Association.

"Surry what?" someone who owned a barking dog said. The selectman cleared his throat.

"Wetlands," he answered.

"And what exactly is that?" the man asked.

Someone helped him out: "That's a word people use when they're not from Surry," he said. I turned around to meet the solid gaze of the men behind us.

"I suppose that means if I've got a 'wetland,'" another said, drawing the word out to the amusement of his friends, "I suppose if I've got this thing you call a 'wetland,' even if I've paid for it and own it, you think your job is to take it away from me. Is that it?"

The selectman stood up behind his metal table. "That's not it. That's not anybody's job," he said. He snatched a piece of paper and read aloud his list on the proper licensing of dogs, the humane treatment of dogs, and noise pollution caused by dogs. But the subject of wetlands suited the men in the back of the room just fine. They let go of the dogs and bit deep into what freedom means to land-owning individuals.

"If the town's planning to take away private land because the state tells them to, and if these people here think that they need to take care of our wetlands for us, I want to know where your rights stop and mine begin.

Tell me that!" another said. His voice hung in the big, high-ceilinged room.

A flush-faced man in the back row bolted upright, and shouted, "Pretty soon we can't even hold a yard sale on our front lawns! We'll get arrested for holding a yard sale!"

No one knew how to respond to this looming threat. We remained dumbfounded and silent.

Then an elderly man came to the rescue. Sitting midway in the lines of chairs, he carefully broke the silence. Turning sideways, he clasped one hand in another and said, "I'd like to know what we're talking about here. Are we talking democracy or communism?"

The selectman cleared his throat and began his introduction to the complexities of dog licensing.

I wanted to stand up and tell them that we work to save what they have tossed away: pieces of marsh and their uplands, thin blades of shore, a few woodlots, fields growing back in alders, a stream or two. In truth, this land is one body. Broken by false boundaries. Scarred. We are not Communists, but, yes, we believe in the self-renewing community between wild land and human beings. We believe in the concept of the wild commons.

Instead, I listened to the facts behind the rising price of licensing.

‌‌⌣

Ray knows, and so do I, that there are places in this town still haunted by the ghosts of wildness, where land flourishes in that complicated relationship with its plants and animals. A person can walk into these few leftover pieces, and, for a time, be the single representative of our species among all the others, and hear, instead of the dominant human cacophony, the sweet relief of other voices.

A month after we burned the brush, Ray rode over on his tractor and plowed my garden. My children were away at school and I was living alone.

"I couldn't live back here all by myself," he told me. "It would make me uneasy."

"I like it," I said.

"I know you do," he said.

A few years after that, when he came to deliver stove

wood he said, "By the way, I've been thinking maybe the work your group there is doing is mostly a good thing. This town is changing too fast."

Ray and I and others whose time on the land in this town has informed our choices and has imparted standards are caught and held by what is disappearing before our eyes. But it is more than that.

We live in a place where land is bought and sold. The field with the view is Ray's retirement savings. Some day he may sell it to a developer, and houses will be built and those houses will cut off what he has looked at every day of his adult life. Driveways will wind down the hill. People will crowd their boats along the long ledge where now the black ducks and an assortment of gulls, arctic and common terns, black-bellied plovers, and spotted sandpipers rest and preen midtide. In a world where land is money, and where our rural labor goes for cheap, what else do we have?

I own an acre on the road, separate from the land where I live. I call it my catastrophe acre. Only a catastrophe will force me to sell it. A flock of turkeys owns it now. In summer, nuthatches nest in holes in the dead tree boles. In spring, spotted salamanders roused from winter slumber climb out from under thick beds of sphagnum to make their slow crawl to the ponds by the house. I pray I will never be trapped between my own needs and this dank patch of wild growth where animals whose needs are simple and clear thrive.

I imagine Ray, on some days—maybe on those crisp dawns when he can see the sun rising above Mount Desert across the flashing water—gets up and feels the same.

Neighborhood Deer

In 1535, Jacques Cartier and his crew, stuck for the winter in the New World, took the advice of a man who was most likely a Micmac and made themselves a tea of northern white cedar. They steeped the sprays and bark into a pungent, resinous brew that saved them from death by scurvy. They called the tree "arbor vitae," tree of life.

In my town, the arbor vitae is the whitetail deer tree. It grows best in acidic bottomlands, where its thickets can persist for centuries, holding back the bite of winter snow and wind. Our neighborhood deer own such a place in the woods across the road from my house. In the sullen, cold afternoons of late winter, they walk through the snow at the back of my yard to their yard, a tamped-down refugium where they settle in for the night.

The tree of life is also their winter food tree. If I want to know how the deer will fare in the hunger season—the long weeks of late winter and early spring—I look for browse lines on the cedars. Around my house, the tansy-scented leaves are hemmed back as far as a deer on a snow bank can reach. They have stolen next winter's food from themselves.

The does and their big fawns gathered under those cedars at the end of last winter to eat the tough green sprays, their skinny legs up to their hocks in the snow, their necks stretched into the branches, their heads hidden. Sometimes one of them would lift onto its back legs to reach into the higher branches. They did not care who watched them from the house, and as the winter wore down, they did not care who came out the door.

Food was what they cared about. They ate in silence.

The only sounds came from the tugs they made at the branches and the sharp and sudden cracks as their hooves broke the crusted snow.

A game trail leads across the paved road to that cedar copse where the deer have their shelter. The trail follows an old dirt road along a narrow esker, then drops to cross a stream that ushers water out of the heath two miles to the north and pours it into the salt marsh a half-mile to the south.

When a forester cut these woods ten years ago, he felled the grand softwoods, limbed, twitched, yarded them, and hauled them away. Now the land grows back in raspberries, in red maple shoots and young fir and pine, cedar and spruce and birch, which is just fine for the deer. The game trail is much older than the cutting. The deer are true to it all year long.

In the evenings, when neighbors and I walk the road, we sometimes see them step out from the trail. Lifting one sharp hoof after another, they walk into full view and stand looking at us before they cross to where the trail picks up on the other side. We count them: three, four, five, six. One or the other of us sometimes can't help lifting a hand to wave, a small gesture of acknowledgment. Of shared community. When the deer see the waving hand, their ears twitch—one, two—as if they were waving back.

We meet the deer like this with the sun shining low on the road, making a soft brushstroke of gold that backlights them as they travel through it and disappear.

One morning in August, at the side of the road, I heard what I thought was rapid, shallow breathing. I stepped in the high grass of the shoulder and almost stumbled into the ditch where the carcass of a deer lay on its side.

It trembled all over as if it were getting its life back in fits and starts. But the life it was tending belonged to thousands of glistening cream-colored maggots that engulfed the body. They writhed, climbing under and over each other a couple of layers thick, gorging on the warm deer flesh. Their bodies chafed, making the wet panting noise I had heard. No place on the corpse was free of these turgid maggots. Even the socket that once held the sleek globe of the left eye was full to overflowing like a cup, and the parts of the deer I could not see, the liver, the lungs, the ruminant stomach, and the heart, were thrumming.

The deer gave itself to the task of becoming something else, which did not look either easy or painful. Some days later, it flew away as blowflies and flesh flies and carrion beetles.

It left a scatter of bones and pieces of stiff skin.

⋎

A neighbor of mine walked onto the deck of his house one early morning just before hunting season with a mug of coffee in his hand, took a sip, and glanced down the cobbles of Patten Bay to the gunmetal water. He looked again. There, up to its belly in the tide, stood a doe. Two coyotes patrolled the beach in front of her. Back and forth they paced over the stones, stopping every now and then to fix her with their eyes. She stood with her head up, frozen in one posture, the water sloshing at her sides.

Alert to every move they made, she did not look directly at them. They looked at her straight on.

My neighbor froze, too. If he made any sound, the smallest gesture, she might bolt shoreward. He stood still until, for no reason he could tell, both coyotes stopped at once. Together they turned to look at him. It may have been a puff of wind carrying his scent, because after the first hard frosts the morning wind blows from the land to the water. Whatever it was, the coyotes pinned him with their gaze. Then they raced into the brush. The doe never moved.

My neighbor took a sip of coffee, which was no longer hot. The doe didn't seem to notice him. Or maybe she discounted his presence. He took another sip. He watched her shift a little in the water that had risen up her belly. Then, slowly, heavily, she waded ashore, stood on the beach, looked both ways.

"What the hell?" my neighbor said to no one as she ran into the brush in the same direction as the coyotes.

"What the hell?"

The apple tree in my yard is a twenty-year-old Northern Spy. After the first hard frost, it begins to drop its big, scabbed, sweet-sour fruit onto the stiff grass.

Today a doe and her fawn took the windfalls into their mouths and crushed them. They stood beneath the tree seriously chewing, jaws moving from side to side, juice splashing their nostrils and pouring down their chins. Their long pink tongues came out and slurped it up. I stood at the window, the imagined tartness of apple watering my own mouth.

Both wore the buff-colored coats of winter. They had gleaming black eyes, gleaming black noses. Their bellies were purest white. Velvet antler buds sprouted between the ears of the yearling above a face that kept some of the round softness of childhood. The doe's head was lean and spare.

When done with apples, they sauntered off, swishing their big, white tails from side to side.

A raven lifted off the bright splash of a gut pile on the snow in a clearing where a hunter had disemboweled a deer. The bird yelled as it flew, circling once over the trees.

I was walking the clearing to the east of the road and came to the green mass of shredded rumen and blood and the loops of intestine yanked by the bird. But there was something else, something I noticed up by the trees. Something tossed aside. I walked over and picked it up. It filled my hands. It was deeply furred, immaculately white. Parting the luxuriant hollow guard hairs, I found two bare testicles as round as reptile eggs, coal black. From them ran a sheath, just the tip of the penis showing beyond it, pink and sharply pointed.

It had been cut from the buck, and, in what seemed a shabby gesture, flung. What should I do with it? Unsure, I held it in my bare hands. In the end, I dug into the loose snow under the trees. When my fingers reached dirt, I made a few scrapes, and carefully laid this purse of unspent coin inside, covered it up, and tamped it in with the soles of my boots as the raven coasted over the trees once more, in silence, dipping a wing toward the gut pile.

⤙

I live on land that has not surrendered the last of its wildness. It keeps secrets, and those secrets prompt us to pay attention, to look for more. This is how we first engaged with the world, and we still do it. We are hungry to know. Wild land and wild animals taught us about themselves, but they also helped make us who we are: resourceful, persistent, with a knack for imagining what we have not seen. Most of the time we catch mere glimpses, and from them we surmise a whole.

Jed Island

Before the developments were built into this land that people had forgotten about for generations, before the roads and driveways went in, I used to cross Spruce Cove at Morgan Bay and cut inland, across one of the many overgrown fields turning back into woodland. I climbed crumbling stone walls pierced by the roots and trunks of black alder and covered in woodbine, and skirted piles of fieldstones covered in rock tripe. In the piles of stones I could feel what I thought was the tiredness of the farmers who hauled and dropped them a hundred and fifty years ago, when the land kept giving them bumper crops of stones in a spring thaw.

I loved to walk, and a number of my neighbors did, too. Although we never discussed it, I think we were people who were letting things in and working things out. Land gone back to wild allowed us to do that.

We didn't know it then, but we were living the final years of an interregnum, between the extended twilight of our rural past and the sudden bright burst of our suburban future. We thought that we were witness to wildness reinventing itself here in what appeared to us to be tracts of common land. We thought we might live to see something of what John Cabot saw, or something of what Samuel de Champlain saw in 1604, when he mapped this coast, its convoluted coves and river mouths and islands.

One place that has not been built on is Jed Island, over two miles straight down Morgan Bay. It sits at the mouth of the bay like a loose cork in a bottle, twelve acres of rock and dirt, red spruce, a few pines, and red oaks with a bald eagles' nest in one of them. Around it flow the tides and the swimming harbor seals and harbor porpoises, the stripers, schools of herring, eels, sail-boats, ducks, gulls, loons, and kayaks.

The great American Luminists, who gave us big places to get lost in, always painted in for their audience a spot somewhere on the canvass of especial brightness or of concentrated dark for the eye to go. They knew that the human eye needs a point of focus. Here, at Morgan Bay, that point is Jed Island.

We look past the undulating mainland shoreline, the rocks and trees now punctuated with houses, to a shimmering island with a razorback line of trees that is empty of people. A destination to dream about. The island is an untamed renegade. We count on it to remind us of the same in ourselves.

On ledges just beyond the island, seals loll at the end of summer, their huge eyes taking in the comings and goings around the harbor of East Blue Hill. They lie on the rough rocks with their rear flippers raised, their heads raised, a gathering of disembodied smiles.

This past summer on one of the island's little coves, I found the body of a young buck, the cups of bone stark between his ears where he had shed his first antlers.

Who knows what drove him here or why he did not dare to swim back to the mainland. Perhaps the winter's ice that reached the island in February imprisoned him. He died just above the high tide line.

He lay down on his side, neatly curled up his front and back legs, and stretched his neck forward on the sand. And that is how I found him, plucked clean of flesh, his bones undisturbed, the posture suggesting a point of focus, a headfirst exit, a long leap into something else.

Cormorants

 I.

I stood on a hill of young poplars that fell steeply to the Union River a half a mile before it empties into the bay. When the tide shifted and the bay water began to roll up to meet the river water coming down, the wind picked up. The poplars, in their new spring green, waved and waved.

Down at the river, the water was dark, as were the banks beneath old overhanging trees. From where I stood, it could have been a deep fissure in the earth, something that fell away from all this happy new brightness, and I remembered, suddenly, the story of Persephone, released for a time from the maw of the underworld, rushing back to this green home and to her mother, Demeter. As I stood on the hill under the trees a man standing up in his boat emerged from the deep shadows of the river and came floating down the water. He waved at me and smiled and his white teeth flashed. In his other hand he held onto the neck of a dead cormorant. His shotgun lay propped against the gunnel.

All spring these double-crested cormorants had worked at the steady, serious business of coming north. I had seen them over the bay water at the horizon, black, long-necked birds flying in an almost endless line like notes on an staff. They are large birds, heavy fliers. Day after day this purposeful march continued where the water met the sky, thirty feet or so above the roll and fetch of the waves. Sometimes the lines of birds veered upward. Sometimes the end of a line moved slowly forward to pass the birds in the lead.

Cormorants are fish eaters. Most of their catch is of little commercial value, but they are opportunistic and gather wherever fish school. They return in time for the smelt runs and the alewife runs, ready to indulge themselves in the extravagant provenance of spring.

In 1899, cormorants became rare nesters along this coast. Only out on the rocks of Black Horse Ledge, in Penobscot Bay, a few viable nests remained, made from kelp strands and rockweed and grasses and gull feathers. The traditional nesting islands had been plundered, the birds' eggs smashed, the birds' bodies used to bait lobster traps and cod hooks. People who made a living on the water had no patience with cormorants feasting in their herring weirs. Sometimes just the presence of the birds in the weirs would cause the trapped fish to pile up against the nets and smother. And then, too often, the birds got stuck in the weave and drowned, and fishermen, checking on their weirs the next day, would find floating, putrefying fish, and dead birds snagged underwater. They would have to pull all the nets up, clean everything out, and start over. They hated cormorants. They called them sea rats.

But the international migratory bird treaties of 1918 and 1936 stopped cormorant killing, except by state permit. The birds rebounded and reclaimed their islands.

Then they began catching farmed fish in the pens set up in our bays. They flourished. Meanwhile, our wild fisheries have dwindled and fallen away.

When the state initiated hatchery programs to reintroduce wild Maine salmon to their traditional rivers, the young fish—called smolts—were hosed into the rivers from tank trucks in the spring. The fish swirled through the hoses and shot out into the wild current where cormorants welcomed them home. Shooting permits, issued by the Department of Marine Resources to defend the hatchery fish, were easy to get for almost anyone, and for years the delicate beauty of the season was shattered by gunshots along our local rivers.

I wanted to find out about the cormorant program on the Union, and called the department to ask how one applies for a permit to kill the birds. The man in charge was a sergeant.

"How do you get one of these?" I asked him.

"You have to be," he said, "a concerned salmon fisherman."

"A what?"

His voice stiffened. "A concerned salmon fisherman," he repeated. "We don't give them out to people who just like to shoot black birds."

"Black birds? You mean the color matters here?"

"I couldn't say, ma'am."

"How do you tell a person who likes to shoot black birds from a concerned fisherman?"

"Ma'am, are you calling because you want to apply for a permit?"

"No," I said.

I watched the fisherman in his boat as he slowly motored downriver to the bay. When he was gone, I walked to the river. In the gently lapping water two dead birds drifted toward the rocks where I grabbed them, one by one, by their wide-palmed feet and lugged them onto the bank. I had brought a knife to cut open any cormorants I found, and I did so, starting between the legs and moving up to the ribs. Above me, a bald eagle flew over, heading upstream. The sergeant had told me the permit required all fishermen who killed cormorants to collect the bodies, open them up, and count the number of salmon smolts inside.

My knife unzipped the first bird. It was still warm. I put my hand in its bloody gut and pulled out an alewife, ten inches long. I felt around for something more, but that was this bird's last meal. I cut the second bird open as the eagle flew over again. One more alewife. In each bird, one flat-sided, silvery alewife, wide-eyed and quite dead. The birds were hunting their spring prey, which they had done for thousands of years before we ever came into this river.

II.

Green Island sits in Pigeon Hill Bay, east of Petit Manan Point. I sat in the stern of a powerboat as we headed out to the island, passing juts of rock sticking up out of the water, one of them busy with cormorants flying to and from it.

I had been assigned to write an article on the controlled tern nesting program on the island initiated that spring. For generations, Green had been a nesting haven for common and Arctic terns before open dumps and effluent pipes caused the herring gull population to explode. The gulls feasted on our refuse in winter; in summer they added tern eggs and chicks to their diets. As the numbers of gulls increased, they took over islands for their own expanding colonies. Green was one of them.

Along this coast, tern islands were becoming alarmingly rare. The College of the Atlantic and the U.S. Fish and Wildlife Department implemented this pilot program on Green to poison gulls before the terns came back in the spring. The gulls were fed a chemical that caused renal failure. They died on or near their nests, folding themselves in like big white dinner napkins.

Immediately, the terns came back and nested. I walked the island with the biologist who oversaw the project, carefully circumventing the nesting areas thick with the delicate, raucous birds bringing food to their young. In the bright, cold afternoon, I walked an outpost of resurgence with its own dark lining.

On the way back, the biologist steered the powerboat toward that nubble of rock with the cormorants. It rose at a distance above the water like a perfect biscuit: crenulated along its sides and flat on top. His assistant, a quiet first-year graduate student in wildlife biology, was looking a little seasick. We drew up beside the island. Double-crested cormorants were flying everywhere as if it were a busy airport. This was one of their nesting islands.

The biologist cut the motor and the boat began to slosh sideways in the wind.

"Here's the problem," he said. I hadn't noticed a problem, but he was about to explain one. "We need to go up on that island before we go back to the dock," he nodded his head toward the cormorants. "The surf is too high for me to go with him," this time he nodded toward the graduate student. "So I am wondering if you would mind taking my place while I keep the boat steady here."

"Take your place for what?" I asked. I noticed a young seal tucked against the rockweed on the island's side.

"We need to pick up ten juvenile cormorants from this island."

"May I ask why?"

"Yes, of course. They need them out in Michigan. There are many toxins in the great lakes and the cormorant young there are hatching with deformities. They need a baseline, some clean cormorants, for their studies."

"But I've read they've already isolated the chemicals that cause the defects," I said. The day was beginning to wear on me. I had witnessed a successful poisoning program that had helped terns, but it was a success borne of a larger failure because the gull population was due to our own excess. Now I just wanted to go home.

"Well, maybe they are doing the tests again," he shrugged his shoulders. "But I said I'd bring some in. You don't have to do this. I suppose I may be able to get out here again tomorrow. It's up to you."

Did I owe him this? He had taken me out on his boat, spent the whole day letting me interview him. Explained the poisoning, the history of tern islands. Now this.

"It sounds like some graduate thesis to me," I told him.

"I have no idea," he said, and waited for my answer.

I had cared for, doctored, and released wild birds for years. But I had also killed the hopelessly sick and injured. I was sitting on that rocking boat trying to figure out how complicit I was in all this business of life and death. But I couldn't make sense of it.

"Okay," I said. I shoved my backpack with my notebook and pencils in the wheelhouse while the biologist and the boy untied an inflatable dinghy. It was red and black and had two yellow oars in plastic locks.

The boy and I put on life jackets, and then they lowered the dinghy over the side of the powerboat. The boy slipped down into it on a rope and snatched up the oars, and then I took the rope down. The biologist leaned over as the boy was churning the oars at the water, trying to keep the little dinghy from sliding under the hull of the bigger boat, and he handed me a laminated cardboard box with a snap top and tiny vents in its sides with "U.S. Fish and Wildlife" stamped in green across it.

Slowly, he swung the big boat away from us and we slapped our way to the island, bobbing over the waves. I held on to the box with both hands, certain I was going to fall into the water, which was splashing frigid sprays over the sides.

The boy headed for the little notch of rock and seaweed where the seal lay, its head up high, watching us approach. At the last moment, it slipped into the water, and the boy turned the dinghy around so that the stern nudged the rock. I threw the box onto the seaweed, jumped out, and tied the painter around a jut of stone. He got out and climbed up the side of the rock as I stood below. As his head rose over the top, adult cormorants took off in a great cloud of panicked flapping. I handed him the box and climbed up behind him.

It was another world. The adults had vanished. I could see their retreating forms at the horizon. All around us were these strange, live things, their bright little eyes on us, their beaks open, their fuzzy charcoal-gray bodies squat in their nests, their little arms that would turn into wings some day hugging their sides. They were darling—as cute as fuzzy toys—and helpless, and they looked at us with an innocence that made me look away.

I'm in hell, I thought. The sky had turned dark. The wind was blowing harder. The water around the island heaved and slapped.

The top of the island was indeed flat but uneven, and in all the cracks and creases were pools of water and excrement with flies swarming above. The smell hit me like a cudgel. I could hardly breath. And then the boy and I began to move toward the baby birds. The biologist had told us exactly what he wanted: some that were quite small, with just the start of fuzz, and some larger ones, which were now moving away from us toward the other edge of the island in a wave. I was terrified they'd go over the side like lemmings, but instead they divided at the edge and scooted along the rim of stone and headed back toward the center.

First I took the little ones who did not move off their nests. They were hot in my hands, and their dark skin was slightly damp. They made no protest nor any sound as I set them in the box. Then for the big ones. We had to chase them down, and once I stepped on the rotting body of a dead chick and it turned into slime under my sneaker. I scooted into one of the fly pools, jumped up, and grabbed a bird. The boy was doing more or less the same. By the time we got to ten, the place was a train wreck of nests and terrified birds. He climbed down to the dinghy and I handed him the box, then I climbed down and we left the island.

I held the box. The young birds were silent, except for a hesitant percussion of uneven tapping of their beaks against the cardboard. Tap-tap. Tap-tap. Tap-tap. They waited in abrupt darkness, with, quite unseen, my arms tight around them. The dinghy lurched and the spray showered us. I pressed the side of my face against the box, and felt the unmistakable weight of shame. I thought of the island now, in chaos, and of these ten sacrificial young birds, and I knew I had done a sharp and penetrating thing.

Rain

A spring peeper sits somewhere in the wisteria at the open window. It is giving its rain call. It has hidden itself in the havoc of leaves, but I know it is about the size of a single wisteria blossom no larger than a penny. I know that when it calls, its tiny, translucent throat pulses like an inflating balloon. The oversized stutter, sharper than a razor stroke, shrieks through the house.

It is late August. It has been raining for three weeks. Yesterday the sun came out and hung in the sky, drying everything out. But before evening a thick fog rolled in smelling of ocean, and by midnight it was raining again. Molds bloom on the wall plaster downstairs like gray chrysanthemums. In the field outside, aphids the color of mahogany attach themselves to the stems of asters. Their mouthparts are deep in the sweet, wet tissues, as if they were drinking from straws. They lift their legs and float them leisurely in the air in what I assume is a gesture of pure pleasure.

Someone walking on the road in a slicker pulls a chipmunk or a red squirrel off the asphalt and the carrion beetles, bright-winged, soft-bellied, dive in and bury themselves in warm flesh.

We're stuck. The gears of the hours have rusted shut. According to the peeper, we're here forever.

On the evening news, we learn that in southern Arizona fires devour the parched landscape. We learn that in the Alps, glaciers are spilling thousands of years of ice down newly exposed rock. In fatal desert places a war goes on.

We have rain. The peeper sounds as if its throat aches, as if it might be about to lose its voice. Rain, rain, rain, rain, it cries. As if we didn't know.

I walked to the bay this evening to get away from the peeper. I sat down in the rank grass and watched a mixed flock of twenty or so semipalmated plovers and semipalmated sandpipers. They were plucking things out of the mud, making tiny jabbing noises with their bills, and from the back of their throats issued plaintive sounds. One bird lifted off the mud with a call like a sweet inflected question, and every other bird flew to join it. They darted away in a tight configuration, flying at a tilt, their white bellies flashing in the dull air.

These birds have seen the arc of the sun move toward the horizon north of here. They have felt the fractions of daylight shrink. They come in here shifting the season, and time races forward, no matter what the peeper says.

The Fire and the Owl

When I drive through my town at night, light pours out of the windows of the houses by the road, and I sometimes see someone move in front of a window, a human silhouette. These people are my neighbors going about the privacy of their lives. The sight reassures and unsettles me. I like knowing the people of my town. But seeing them like this, backlighted and silent, brings to my mind a person's essential solitariness, and the thought that we will always be, in small or large ways, strangers to each other.

Last winter a house set up on cinder blocks out on

Toddy Pond Road, six miles from where I live, ignited. It stood in a pinched clearing in the woods, twenty yards or so off the hardtop, attached to the road by a trail through the ragged softwood trees.

The quick midnight burn must have roared like a drumroll as it grew. It must have spangled the snow as it ate up the house. Then it died and no one in the houses or trailers nearby heard it or smelled it. If one of the dogs inside the engulfed home barked, the sound was lost. By dawn no trace of soot hung in the air, no plume of telltale smoke lifted into the sky. People got up the next morning and looked out their windows to a steady snowfall.

Allen, the owner of the local general store, noticed that the man didn't stop in for his morning coffee. He wasn't standing on the wet wood floor with snow boots dripping and his railroad cap pushed down on his head and gloves hanging from the pockets of his open jacket. More than a few men in this town start their day at the store, talking to each other about this or that. When they finish their coffee and the talk winds down, they get back in their pickups and drive to work.

An hour later, Allen noticed that the man's wife hadn't shown up with their son, a twenty-two-year-old boy, mild-tempered but a bit disengaged, the way some people get when their lives have narrowed to trips to the hospital, and they have learned to count on the help of people they barely know. The neighbor who had volunteered to drive them yesterday sat in her car in the parking lot of the store with the heater going. She was waiting to take them to Bangor, an hour away, for the boy's dialysis.

Allen asked her to wait some more. He hopped into his car and drove up the Toddy Pond Road and took a look at the place between the trees where the path starts up. He saw that the snow was unbroken. He drove back and called the police. The night of the fire, before the snow fell, a friend and I got into her car and drove to the dance class we take together once a week in Belfast, a town also an hour away. This time of year we drive in the dark both ways. In the big, mirrored studio we dance to an African drummer, loosen the tight boundaries of ourselves with the help of the drums, and emerge from the class exhausted and cleansed, for a time, of small troubles.

As we drove to the class, the headlights of my friend's car threw spare yellow cones forward onto the blacktop of Route 15. They made a narrow frame to see by, especially in farm country like this, with fields on either side, and unlit barns.

A tawny whir of feathers flared into the lights. The owl slapped the right fender and somersaulted toward the snow bank at the road's shoulder. My friend was shocked, still driving, her mouth open.

"Shit," she whispered.

"Turn around," I told her. "I think we can find it."

We went back half a mile. Everything looked the same: the flat stretch of snowbound fields, the crusted snowpack on the shoulder, the whiskery brush beyond it. We couldn't tell where we had struck the owl. I got out and stepped into the snow. She flicked the brights on and drove the car a few feet behind me. The wind was blowing. I followed the edge of the field, breaking the crust with my pack boots. My eyes combed the brush and scanned the snow. But I saw nothing. I came to the end of the field, and we started on the next one, and then I came to the end of that one.

Maybe the owl had simply flown away. Maybe it was close by and I couldn't see it. I scanned the snow again, wanting it to appear, wanting to hold it in my sight, to lift it up and let it fly away, or to take it and try to heal it. But I saw nothing. I stood listening. All I heard was the wind.

Then I got back into the car and my friend drove us to dance class. We didn't say much. I didn't feel much like dancing after that, and maybe she didn't either. I asked her if the owl seemed big or small to her. She said small. I told her I thought it was a saw-whet. I didn't tell her I was pretty sure that if it had not gotten up and flown off, it was still alive somewhere on the snow behind us.

While the new snow started to fall outside, we danced. I think it may have been at about the time the fire first set a spark to the house on cinder blocks. Maybe some coals festering in the old clothes behind the woodstove where the four dogs slept started it, or a flare-up of creosote turning the stovepipe red. We danced and they died and all night the snow fell.

A neighbor phoned the next morning to tell me about the fire. By mid-morning the police had sorted out the bodies of the man and his wife and their son and the dogs. Remind me who they are, I ask my neighbor. Oh, he answers, and his voice is tired, you've seen them a hundred times.

I don't remember them, I say.

I must have stood beside them at the elementary school softball games where our daughters played, for they had two daughters, grown and living somewhere else, as mine is. I must have walked right by the boy when I picked up my son and daughter at school.

My children live in cities now. They call on the weekends, and today I ask each of them if they remember this family. And they do. The images of the three people come easily to their minds, because they are a part of my children's stories of growing up in this small town. My daughter remembers the boy humming a tune he liked to himself. It was a sound that seemed to give him comfort. She remembers the cloudy thickness of his old-fashioned glasses. My son tells me about the pressed and formal and threadbare clothes the mother wore. He says "threadbare," and I can tell it hurts him to confess the word's accuracy. Then he says that when the school bus left the boy off at the head of the path, it looked as if he turned into a child in a folktale. The bus would pull away as my son watched this small figure step between the trees and disappear.

I go outside to split kindling and bring in dry wood. I start the fire in the stove and go out for more wood. The smoke curls up from the chimney into the snow coming down, steady and thick.

When you live in a small town, you meet people at school, at the general store, the man who sells lobsters and clams in summer down at the dock on Newbury Neck, the woman who sells flowers out of a tiny, pretty building that was once the town post office, the couple who have started an organic farm on the top of the hill above the bay. We are joined in time and place. Sometimes we attend town functions and someone tells a story of the people who came before us and made community here. We listen and hope that our little group may provoke a story or two, and that our stories will linger, imparting a moment of tragedy or courage, humor or grief or joy, or even a spate of passing foolishness. Our stories say we were here. We made a difference to each other. We cared.

And this is how we carry what we know of the past into the future.

🏵 Epilogue

When my children were young, I met a man in a nearby town who took care of injured and orphaned wild birds, and he had the stern, reticent kindness to teach me. When he thought I knew enough to start, he gave me a young robin. I was to raise it because it was orphaned. Not only that, I was to introduce it to its natural wild life.

It was still downy, but even then, it was an especially dark bird, unlike most robins in this part of the country. It was more like the birds that fly past us to nest much farther north in the spring and who come back through in the fall. Dark, bold birds. Birds of the taiga.

My children and I decided that this robin was a female, although we knew that males are darker than females. Despite this, we called her Clarissa.

After eating, Clarissa settled down in the nest we made for her, uttering high, soft sounds. She liked those sounds returned. My children and I learned to make them back to her, and she replied. It was a language between us, pre-verbal and absolutely clear in intent. Clarissa also wanted a little contact before she slept, a little petting. She let us know this by stirring about in her nest until, gently, so as not to harm her crisp forthcoming feathers, we drew a clean washed finger from the top of her head down her back and she would close her eyes, and we would pet her, listening to her sounds grow fainter until she slept.

She got bigger. She hopped around the room where we kept her, hopped onto us, pulled our hair, gently pecked at our ears and noses. She seemed to enjoy and trust us, although she knew we were not robins. When she started to fly, which we could not do with her, she would aim at our heads and shoulders.

We were lucky. It was all new, and Clarissa never got sick. She never had an accident or injury. Soon she was flying free. We still fed her, and we followed her into the garden to watch her chase down insects and yank worms.

Then the man who had become my teacher and guide—who was showing me his way of making a good life for himself—offered us three more orphaned robins. We raised them. And so did Clarissa. We brought them outside in their handmade nest and when she heard their hunger cries, she flew in and fed them, too. She brought them wild food, and often she plucked up the mush we held in a bowl and stuffed that down their throats. When they grew up, they flew off with her.

We called to them in the morning. They answered from behind the trees and flew in their little energetic flock to the porch where we fed them. They knew how to feed themselves by then. It was a gesture of attachment, I assumed, and soon they outgrew it.

We succeeded. The price of success was seeing these four, each a distinct personality, take off into the world that was larger than these gardens and scrub edges, this ring of trees and spring pools. It was this larger world that had brought them here.

To grow up they needed something from us. To raise them well, we needed something from them. Whatever word we choose to name this communion between species—whatever sounds we make to say it—it is both fearless and gentle and it not only enriches lives, it saves them.